on scre

Monty
Python

the complete guide

Steve Pilkington

sonicbondpublishing.com

Sonicbond Publishing Limited
www.sonicbondpublishing.co.uk
Email: info@sonicbondpublishing.co.uk

First Published in the United Kingdom 2020
First Published in the United States 2020

British Library Cataloguing in Publication Data:
A Catalogue record for this book is available from the British Library

ISBN 978-1-78952-047-7

Typeset in ITC Garamond & ITC Avant Garde
Printed and bound in England

Graphic design and typesetting: Full Moon Media

on screen ...

Monty Python

Contents

Acknowledgements
Thanks firstly to Stephen Lambe for his unswerving loyalty
to the books I keep presenting him with.
Sometimes even after he has read them.

Thanks also to Janet for enduring and even indulging in a
seemingly endless stream of Python televisual material. Python is
seldom best watched alone!

Most of all, thanks to the six core Pythons (plus associated Snake-
ettes, Cleveland, Innes et al) for leaving us with a priceless legacy
which changed the face of comedy forever. No it didn't. Yes it did.
No it didn't! 'Ping!' Thank you, good morning! Your time is up...

Introduction

Python Origins

'Monty Python'. Like 'The Beatles', 'Pink Floyd' or 'Led Zeppelin' it's become a brand ingrained into the thread of popular culture – much bigger than its origins as a surreal, anarchic TV comedy show, much like the band names above have evolved far beyond their origins as psychedelic pioneers, guitar-led beat group or blues-influenced heavy rock band. At any given moment, you can safely say that someone, somewhere is quoting a line from *Life Of Brian, Holy Grail* or one of the many, many TV sketches which have entered our shared consciousness. It hardly even matters whether they are quoted accurately, as it is the intent and spirit of them which makes them live so vibrantly.

Who *were* the five Englishmen and one American who made up the original *Python* troupe, however? Before we take a look at how they came together and developed their shared chemistry, let's take a look back at their beginnings.

John Cleese, perhaps the most famous and recognisable of the Pythons, was born John Marwood Cleese in Weston-Super Mare in October 1939. He made his appearance just as the Second World War was being declared, which maybe should have come as something of a hint. The family name was originally Cheese, which they believed – quite rightly, to be fair – sounded somewhat ridiculous, so they changed it around the time of the First World War. Which, ironically, was one of the few times that announcing your name as Cheese would, as a matter of fact, be quite likely not to raise a laugh. As a child, John supported local football club Bristol City FC, which was excellent training for the disappointments which life had to throw at him, and as a schoolboy he excelled at boxing and, especially, cricket. He was already over six feet tall at the age of 13, which would have made him stand out somewhat at his school assembly and, one would imagine, encouraged his early love of comedy. Indeed, there is a story that he displayed this latent ability quite early on, when he allegedly painted footprints leading to and from the school statue of Field Marshal Haig, giving the impression that the great man had stepped down from his plinth and gone to the toilet. Having done well at A-Level, the young Cleese was offered a place at Cambridge University but was unable to take it up for two years as the ending of National Service had produced a figurative log-jam of applicable students. When he later married his future *Fawlty Towers* collaborator Connie Booth in Manhattan in 1968, the couple attempted, as an exercise, to remove all religious terminology altogether from their bespoke version of the wedding service. He later recalled that, to his enormous disappointment, a single reference to 'God' crept in near the end, putting quite a damper on proceedings. God was unavailable for comment.

Michael Palin – whose quiet, unassuming presence is often cited as hiding the true soul of the *Python* collective – was born Michael Edward Palin in Sheffield, in May 1943, by which time the worldwide confrontation ushered in by the birth of Cleese had been raging for four years. His first acting experience came at the age of five when, in a somewhat liberal stroke of casting, he played Martha Cratchit in a school performance of *A Christmas Carol*. Undeterred by this experience, he continued to perform. After moving to Oxford University in 1962, to study modern history, he began writing and performing comedy material in earnest. His very first television job came in 1965 for Television Wales And The West, presenting what is described as a 'comedy pop show' entitled *Now!*, of which no record appears to survive, which is almost certainly a very good thing.

Terry Jones, the regular writing partner of Palin, was born in Colwyn Bay, North Wales, in February 1942, carrying the lofty full title Terence Graham Parry Jones. His father was stationed in India with the RAF and, at the age of four, Jones moved with the family to Surrey. He began studying English at Oxford, where he was to meet Palin, but as he puts it 'strayed into history' after becoming interested in the medieval period while studying Chaucer for his degree. Bizarrely, in 1968 he collaborated with Palin as lyricists on an album by Barry Booth, who is remembered by literally dozens. The record, which was reissued in 2002 and of which samples can be found online, has some considerable, whimsical pop-psychedelic charm.

Graham Chapman appeared in January 1941, in Leicester, the son of a policeman. Graham Arthur Chapman, to give him his full title, was raised in nearby Melton Mowbray, where he went to school before studying medicine at Cambridge and then graduating as a medical doctor from St Bartholomew's Hospital Medical College. As a child, he displayed a love of amateur dramatics, including a much-praised role as Mark Anthony in Shakespeare's *Julius Caesar*, and along with his elder brother John, he was an avid fan of radio comedy such as *The Goon Show* while growing up. He died in 1989 from Tonsil Cancer at the age of 48, the first of the Pythons to pass away.

Eric Idle, another wartime *Python* arrival, was born in South Shields, County Durham, in May 1943, the northernmost *Python* by birth. He and his mother had been evacuated to the North East during the war, while his father, having survived RAF service during the conflict, in a cruel twist of fate, was killed in a road accident while hitch-hiking home at Christmas 1945 – this at a time when traffic was still extremely sparse on British roads. Brought up by his mother, the young Idle spent part of his time in Wallasey, on the Wirral, attending school there until he enrolled as a boarding pupil at the Royal Wolverhampton School, which was a charitable foundation dedicated to helping orphans and the children of single parents. Despite these loftily charitable claims, Idle claimed the school was a most unpleasant environment, both physically and mentally, and that to make life tolerable, his outlets were developing a love of subversive comedy, listening to Radio Luxembourg and following Wolverhampton Wanderers, who at that time were a major force in English football. A somewhat militant youth, he was a supporter of the Campaign For Nuclear Disarmament and attended the annual Aldermaston march. Despite this, he did achieve the role of prefect, followed by Head Boy. He was stripped of these titles following

his discovery at a local cinema watching an X-Rated film while underage.
Finally in the *Python* roll-call, comes the sole American - animator Terry
Gilliam. Born Terrence Vance Gilliam in Minneapolis, in November 1940, the
son of a travelling coffee salesman (that is to say, it was his father who was
travelling, not the coffee). By the early 1950s, the family were living in Los
Angeles, where Gilliam had an exemplary school career, being a straight-A
student, class president, senior prom king and voted 'most likely to succeed'.
Around this golden era in his life, he began to become addicted to the satirical
Mad Magazine, an interest which ensured his future downfall, or success,
however one wishes to judge such criteria. He grew his hair and began an
interest in political and social agendas, saying later that he drove around in
a small Hillman Minx car in which he was regularly pulled over and accused
of being a 'long-haired drug addict' by the somewhat over-zealous LA police
of the time. Realising that, despite the burning social unrest he felt, he was a
better cartoonist than social rebel, he left the powder-keg Californian scene in
the mid-1960s to come to England, where he met several other like-minded
social outcasts and ne'er-do-wells, and ultimately became a Python. In 1968
he obtained British Citizenship, holding dual nationality until 2006, when he
renounced his American citizenship, claiming in a newspaper interview that this
was as a protest against then-President George W Bush. Recent years have seen
the world media keen to announce his death, regardless of the facts. In 2015,
Variety magazine published his obituary, despite him being very much alive and
able to read the magazine, while three years later a ruptured artery in his spine
was gleefully seized upon by the world's press corps as being a stroke. Despite
these reports, he continues to be alive and kicking at time of writing.

The Union Of The Snake: Pre-Python activities

The seeds of what would become perhaps the most influential comedy team
in history were sown in the fertile soil of the English University system in
the 1960s. Michael Palin and Terry Jones met at Oxford (where Eric Idle also
attended, slightly later) while John Cleese and Graham Chapman met up on
the other side of the Varsity fence at Cambridge.

All would go on to do work in television prior to *Python*, in various
combinations and as both writers and participants. The first collaborative
venture for the BBC, however, was *I'm Sorry, I'll Read That Again* on the radio.
Beginning in 1964, it featured Cleese, Idle and Chapman on writing duties,
with Cleese also a cast member. This was followed by the team's first foray into
television in 1967, with *The Frost Report*, which saw Palin and Jones join the
others on the writing team and Cleese in front of the cameras. Two more short-
lived TV productions began and ended that year, with Palin and Jones on *Twice
A Fortnight* and the other three on the slightly better remembered *At Last The
1948 Show* both lasting just that single year.

The most successful pre-*Python* project to date began in 1967, with Idle,
Palin and Jones teaming up for ITV's *Do Not Adjust Your Set*. This ran until

1969 to some acclaim, with the programme also featuring animation by Terry Gilliam, whom Cleese had met in New York while on tour with the presciently-named Cambridge Footlights Revue entitled *Cambridge Circus* (in true *Python* fashion this had originally gone under the unlikely billing of *A Clump Of Plinths*). Also appearing on *Do Not Adjust Your Set* was future Python 'extra man' Neil Innes with his group of the time the Bonzo Dog Doo-Dah Band. 1968 brought two more brief excursions onto the television, with Idle and Gilliam both contributing to *We Have Ways Of Making You Laugh*, which unfortunately did no such thing, while Cleese and Chapman wrote *How To Irritate People* (which ironically seems to have done just that to the audience), in which Palin appeared as a cast member.

The time was getting close for the soon-to-be Pythons to unite, when ITV offered Palin, Jones, Idle and Gilliam their own late-night show following the success of *Do Not Adjust Your Set*. However, owing to a delay in having a studio ready to accommodate the project, they lost out on the deal – comedy's own 'turning down the Beatles moment' in its way. After another brief and glorious failure with the little-remembered *Complete And Utter History Of Britain*, Palin was invited by Cleese to join himself and Chapman for a show they had been offered by the BBC. Cleese remembered enjoying working with Palin on the doomed *How To Irritate People*, and the story goes that he wanted a third man owing to the often difficult and unstable personality of Chapman – a fact borne out by Palin's later stories of the latter's mood swings and other issues in his exhaustive *Python Years* diary. Having agreed to join, Palin initiated a domino-like progression as he suggested bringing in Jones and also Idle, who himself had the idea of bringing Gilliam on board. Whatever the exact truth of these circumstances, the team were now in place and only needed a name. The word 'only' is used here advisedly as this prompted some lengthy procrastination...

Snakes Alive: The Pythons get together

The pre-*Python* names for the nascent troupe are as many as they are bizarre. The most widely reported name was *Owl Stretching Time*, which was immortalised when it was chosen as the title of an episode in the first series of the TV show, but there was a wide range of other temporarily adopted titles. These included such surrealistic delights as *The Toad Elevating Moment, Vaseline Review, Ow! It's Colin Plint, The Nose Show, The Algy Banging Hour* and the truly bizarre *A Horse, A Spoon And A Bucket*. According to Michael Palin's fascinating and exhaustive diaries, when the first series of the show began filming the title in place was actually *Bun, Wackett, Buzzard, Stubble and Boot* – a fictional forward line from a Cleese football monologue – but this, one, like many others, failed to amuse the increasingly exasperated BBC. In fact, the powers that be at the BBC were supposedly responsible for the 'Flying Circus' part of the title, as they insisted that they had printed it in their schedules and there could be no more changes.

While this tactic – one step away from actually saying 'Stop this! It's too silly!'

– was partially successful, our heroes still had to agree on who the proprietor of said Flying Circus should be (note: a 'Flying Circus' referred to an aerobatic stunt display team in the first half of the 20th century). Suggestions for this included *Gwen Dibley's Flying Circus* (named after a random woman Palin had read about in a newspaper), *Baron Von Took's Flying Circus* (an amalgam of comedy writer Barry Took and WW1 flying ace Baron Von Richtofen) and the absurd if oddly brilliant *Arthur Megapode's Flying Circus*. Finally, at a suggestion from Idle, *Monty* was decided upon (either as a reference to Field Marshal Montgomery or a man who drank in Idle's local pub, according to which account you read), and put together with the 'slippery sounding' surname *Python* to triumphant effect.

Things were not yet quite settled, however, as the BBC – who one would think would be desperate for this whole farce to be over – decided they didn't like the name and refused it. The team then announced that they were going to change the title of the programme every week until the BBC relented and allowed them to use the title they wanted. One can only assume that the last vestiges of patience and will to live dissipated from the broadcasting powers-that-be at this point, as *Monty Python's Flying Circus* was finally waved through as the name, and history was made.

Series One

All episodes produced by Ian MacNaughton (except Episodes 1-4 produced by John Howard Davies, Episode 6 produced by Ian MacNaughton and Irving C Salzberg) All Episodes directed by Ian MacNaughton (except episodes 1-5 directed by Ian MacNaughton and John Howard Davies)

The exterior location shots for this first series were largely shot in July and August 1969, on the South Coast and other locations in the South of England, though more scenes were shot later. The interior shots which made up the majority of the material were recorded between August 1969 and January 1970. Note that this meant they were still filming as the shows were being broadcast, on a sort of rolling schedule. Audience figures for the shows averaged at around three million, which for a new programme at 11:10 pm on Sundays on BBC2 (the BBC's second channel, which was intended for a more rarified audience and thus received lower viewing figures) was quite remarkable.

Note that series producer and director Ian MacNaughton directed the film sequences only for the first five episodes. Thereafter, he became sole director.

Episode One: Whither Canada?

First aired 5 October 1969
Sketches include:
It's Wolfgang Amadeus Mozart
Famous Deaths
Italian Lesson
Whizzo Butter
Arthur 'Two Sheds' Jackson
Picasso/Cycling Race
The Funniest Joke in the World

Synopsis

The episode begins with the first appearance of Palin as the 'It's' man, as he emerges from the sea, in tattered clothes, similar to Robinson Crusoe. Eventually, he reaches dry land, and as he is about to collapse manages the word 'It's...', only to be abruptly cut off by the theme music and Gilliam's animation sequence, with the giant foot seen for the first time.

The first sketch has a false opening, as an announcer (Chapman) walks on to sit at a desk, saying 'Good evening'. As he sits, we hear a pig squeal, whereupon he crosses off one in a series of pig drawings on a blackboard. At this point, the sketch begins with Cleese as Mozart playing the piano. He then announces that we will be seeing famous deaths, and announces the first as Genghis Khan. We cut to see footage of the legendary warlord keeling over outside his tent, whereupon three judges hold up marks as if judging ice skating. We see a leaderboard before a viewer request for the death of Mr Bruce Foster from Guildford shows him dying theatrically in an armchair, and the final scene shows the famous death of Lord Nelson, with the great man plummeting from an upstairs window in a block of flats. A pig is heard squealing as he lands.

The scene then cuts to Jones as a teacher in an Italian language class, turning away from the window and crossing off another pig. All of the students in the class are, in fact, Italians, who speak English with a heavy accent before translating each other for the teacher. The exception to this is Chapman who stands up to ask a question in Bavarian hat and lederhosen, whereupon he is directed to the German class. An animated commercial for 'Whizzo butter' then airs, followed by a live tasting in which a crowd of housewives claim to be unable to tell the difference between Whizzo and a dead crab.

A fairly lengthy sequence follows with a fictional programme called 'It's The Arts', which, we are told, will, later on, be featuring Picasso attempting a painting while riding a bicycle along various A-roads between Chichester and Battersea. First, however, we see an interview with an esteemed film director named Sir Edward Ross. Cleese, as the interviewer, makes great play of asking whether he objects to being called Edward, before then shortening it to Ted. Both of these are fine, but Sir Edward objects when he then refers to him as 'Eddie Baby', followed swiftly by 'sweetie', 'sugar plum', 'pussycat', and 'angel drawers', and finally 'Frank', which is also declined despite that fact that we discover Sir Robin Day has a hedgehog called Frank. We cut to another studio where the famous composer Arthur Jackson is being interviewed, with much focus on the fact that his nickname is 'Two sheds', although he only possesses one. He becomes annoyed at the obsession with this, culminating when questions about his music are accompanied by a back-projection of a shed. The final segment shows the Picasso bicycle painting, with live coverage from Idle and Cleese along the route. After many other artists hurtle past Cleese painting, culminating in Toulouse Lautrec on a tricycle, we learn that Picasso fell off his bicycle on the B2127 while attempting a short cut to Guildford, and that 'the pig has a slight headache'.

A Gilliam animated sequence featuring characters from largely Victorian photographs behaving very strangely is cut short by the arrival of a large pig, whereupon we cut to a war room with generals pushing pig figures around on a map. The following sketch details the wartime writing of a joke so hilarious that anyone reading or hearing it will die laughing. The joke is translated one word at a time to German and weaponised by British troops reading it aloud. The sketch and the show ends with a memorial to 'The Unknown Joke' in a field and the 'It's' man returning to the sea.

Trivia.

The dead pigs are a running joke throughout the episode, with the final score at the end announced as 'Pigs 9, British Bipeds 4'

The episode is titled 'Whither Canada?', despite there being no reference whatsoever to Canada. It has been reported that this was a suggestion for the series name.

The famous giant foot in the title scene comes from a painting by 16th Century artist Agnolo Bronzino entitled *Venus, Cupid, Folly and Time*.

The full leaderboard of famous deaths consists of St Stephen, Richard III, Joan Of Arc, Marat, Abraham Lincoln, Genghis Khan and Edward VII. The death of Genghis was filmed in Poole, Dorset.

During the 'funniest joke' sketch, the joke is heard being told in German, but the actual meaning is nonsensical with many words being invented. As at the time of writing, Google Translate contains an in-joke whereby if one enters the text of the joke in German, it comes back as 'Fatal Error'. Germany's 'V-joke', created in reprisal, is the weak 'Zwei peanuts vere valking down the strasse. One vas assaulted... peanut', which was broadcast on the radio to no avail. The footage of Hitler in the sketch is taken from a 1935 Nazi propaganda film called The Triumph Of The Will. The sketch may well take its inspiration from a US comic Strip Li'l Abner which, in 1967, ran a lengthy story concerning a joke causing people to die laughing.

Carol Cleveland is credited with appearing in this episode, but she does not appear to take any part in it.

The brand name 'Whizzo' would appear intermittently in future episodes.

Author's Pick.
A very strong first episode, without a true weak link, the choice of funniest sketch is a hard one, which I would put as a tie between the 'Funniest Joke' and the less celebrated 'Picasso Cycling'. Certainly, the classic moments of the policemen intoning a lament as the Inspector enters the house to retrieve the joke, and Toulouse Lautrec going past on a child's tricycle, are both pure genius.

Episode Two: Sex And Violence
First aired 12 October 1969
Sketches include:
Flying Sheep
A Man With Three Buttocks
Musical Mice
Marriage Guidance Counsellor
The Wacky Queen
Working Class Playwright
The Wrestling Epilogue
The Mouse Problem

Synopsis:
The episode opens once again with the 'It's' man, this time struggling over grassy dunes to a beach, to utter his single word. The opening sketch sees Jones, as a tourist, joining a local shepherd (Chapman) looking over a fence at sheep which, we learn, are in the trees, somewhat unusually. This, Chapman

explains, is because being rather dim creatures, they have become obsessed with the idea that they are in fact birds, even though they 'do not so much fly, as plummet'. This is the work of an intelligent sheep named Harold, who is attempting an escape plan. We then see Cleese and Palin as two bizarre Frenchmen demonstrating the benefits of sheep-based aviation.

We next meet Cleese interviewing a man with three buttocks, who refuses to demonstrate this quality, followed by a man with two noses. There is also later mention of a man with nine legs, but we are told that he ran away. This leads to the Musical Mice routine, where Jones plays a sadistic performer who plays the 'mouse organ', consisting of mice trained to squeak different notes strapped to a board, which he hits with two giant mallets, playing *The Bells Of St Mary* before Jones is dragged away, protesting.

Following this is the well known 'Marriage Guidance Counsellor' sketch, which features the first appearance of Carol Cleveland as the glamorous wife of mild-mannered Arthur Pewtey (Palin), who is openly seduced by the counsellor (Idle) during their conversation. They head behind a screen to undress while Pewtey is ushered out, before being sent back in by a cowboy, played by Cleese, telling him to 'be a man'. This fails to work, and he is hit on the head with a chicken by a fully armoured knight (Gilliam), as a caption announces 'So much for pathos!'

This takes us to a bizarre silent film slapstick pastiche, with black and white footage of Queen Victoria and William Gladstone performing practical jokes on each other, narrated by Alfred Lord Tennyson on a wax cylinder recording. We are ushered straight to a living room with Chapman in working-class dress and accent to match, being visited by his son who, in an inversion of the normal cliché, has left his home in Hampstead to go to the bright lights of Barnsley to be a coal miner. This enrages his playwright father, who dismisses him for running away from 'a real day's work', before being stricken by writer's cramp.

A brief Epilogue parody depicting a cardinal and an atheist wrestling to decide the existence of God, leads to the final sketch The Mouse Problem, with Cleese shame-facedly describing he and his friends dabbling in a shadowy world where people secretly dress up as mice. As a clear parody of issues around homosexuality prevalent at the time, it is both brilliantly observed and also very funny.

Trivia.

This episode saw the first appearance of not only Carol Cleveland, but also of Gilliam's chicken-wielding knight, Palin's down-trodden Arthur Pewtey and Cleese and Palin's two Frenchmen sharing one moustache, all of whom would feature multiple times in the future.

The combatants in the wrestling Epilogue are played by two, real-life professional wrestlers.

The opening 'Flying Sheep' sketch leads to a running joke with sheep being shot down during the episode.

An audience of middle-aged women (filmed at a Women's Institute meeting) is shown enthusiastically applauding several announcements, but at one point after a sheep is shot down it is replaced by an audience of Indian women in stony silence.

There are three Gilliam animated sequences in this episode, including the Rodin statue The Thinker disappearing when its thought bubble 'I think therefore I am' is popped. There are more flying sheep, a carnivorous baby in a pram and another Rodin statue, The Kiss, featuring a leg with holes played like a flute.

Finally, the Mouse Problem show *The World Around Us* uses the same Rachmaninoff theme music as *Panorama*, which it clearly parodies. When originally shown, the phone number of Cleese's character was displayed, which in reality was the number of David Frost's production company. This was removed on further screenings after a large number of phone calls were received by Frost. The actual filming of the Mouse sketch was done in Barnes, London on a sweateringly hot day, which Palin recounts as being very uncomfortable in the mouse suits!

Author's Pick.
Not quite as strong as the first episode, with some sequences including the Frenchmen and the 'Epilogue' dragging a little, the strongest sketch here is the brilliant 'Working Class Playwright', which turns expected convention on its head, hilariously.

Episode Three: How to Recognise Different Types of Trees From Quite a Long Way Away

First aired 19 October 1969
Sketches include:
The Larch
Court Scene with Cardinal Richelieu
Bicycle Repair Man
Children's Stories
Restaurant Sketch
Seduced Milkmen
Stolen Newsreader
Nudge Nudge

Synopsis:
After an opening wherein the 'It's' man emerges from a wooded area accompanied by the sound of a lion, and a brief slide referencing recognising a tree ('The Larch', beginning a running joke), we are into a surreal courtroom scene with Eric Idle (Mr Larch, naturally) in the dock. After he delivers a rousing and impassioned speech about freedom, we learn that it is only a

parking offence. The prosecutor, Cleese, then calls a series of bizarre witnesses including a gossiping woman, a dead man in a coffin and Cardinal Richelieu, who is revealed to be a professional Richelieu impersonator. Inspector Dim Of The Yard (Chapman) informs us in song and dance that he would like to be a window cleaner, while Cleese follows suit about being an engine driver. The 'Bicycle Repair Man' sketch sees a world populated by men in Superman costumes in which one of them can transform into his alter ego as 'Bicycle Repair Man', able to repair a bicycle with his bare hands to the astonishment of the Supermen. The narrator, Cleese, is shown at the end in his garden launching into an anti-Communist rant in a clear precursor to his Basil Fawlty character.

We cut from there to Idle as a children's storyteller, reading stories which all quickly become obscene. This sketch is bookended by some bizarre Gilliam animation showing some happy dancing rabbits who get flattened by an intruding hippo. From there we have a short sketch with milkman Palin being beckoned upstairs by a sexy woman and ushered into a bedroom, which contains more milkmen of increasing age and beard lengths, and one skeleton.

We then cut to a restaurant where Chapman and Carol Cleveland are enjoying a very civilised meal, before Chapman casually mentions a dirty fork. This ushers in an escalating series of over-reactions which sees the dishwashing staff fired, the manager stabbing himself to death with the fork and Cleese's enormous cook attacking the diners with a machete. Bookending this is Idle on a beach, where a sign reading 'Donkey Rides' sees two men carrying a donkey (stuffed). After a scene in which a BBC TV newsreader is wheeled away, desk and all, and transported on a lorry (still reading the news) before being pushed into the sea, we are finally treated to Eric Idle's famous 'Nudge Nudge', in which he makes a series of ever more suggestive remarks to Terry Jones' respectable character in a pub.

Comments.
This episode title, the longest in *Python* history, unusually bears some relevance to the content, by way of a running joke in which we are shown how to recognise several types of tree, all of which are 'the larch', apart from a solitary horse chestnut.

Idle's impassioned speech in the courtroom is, in fact, an amalgam of mainly Shakespearian references, specially written for the show. Among others, *The Tempest* and *Julius Caesar* are quoted. Cleese's prosecutor appears to be Jewish for no apparent reason, as per his searching for a 'Kosher car park' and other comments. The clerk of the court is played by the prolific TV writer Ian Davidson, who appeared in eight *Python* episodes in all.

The attractive blonde woman in the 'Milkmen' sketch is often - wrongly - assumed to be Carol Cleveland, as the actress does resemble her. In fact, it is an actress named Thelma Taylor, who had small parts in such things as *Carry On Cleo* and *Benny Hill* in the 1960s. No-one seems to know why she appeared rather than Cleveland, who plays the same part in *And Now For Something Completely Different*. Cleveland does appear in the Restaurant Sketch, yet she is uncredited.

The location where the newsreader is pushed into the sea is the end of Southwold Pier, in Suffolk. Most of the news items refer to Wales, with the exception of one which oddly places Omsk and Krakow together, when in fact one is in Russia and the other in Poland. The cricket report claims that Glamorgan were all out for 36 and yet beat Yorkshire by an innings and seven runs, which seems unfeasible.

The donkey being carried on the beach was filmed at Shell Bay, near Poole in Dorset. Two men, one in this scene, are seen being hit on the head with the chicken in this episode.

According to Idle in the *Rutles* DVD bonus features, Elvis Presley was, in fact, a fan of *Monty Python*, and bizarrely 'Nudge Nudge' was his favourite *Python* sketch.

Author's Pick.
The material here is all strong, yet without a standout classic sketch to be an obvious highlight. My pick would probably be Bicycle Repair Man, if only for its *Batman* type sound-effect captions ('Clink!', 'Screw!', 'Inflate!', 'Adjust Saddle!'). 'Milkmen' is one of the few *Python* sketches to lose impact once the punchline is known, as, very publicly, they eschewed traditional punchlines in general.

Episode Four: Owl Stretching Time
First aired 26 October 1969
Sketches include:
Art Gallery
It's a Man's Life in the Modern Army
Undressing in Public
Self-Defence Against Fresh Fruit
Secret Service Dentists

Introduced by the 'It's' man falling off a high cliff then crawling across a beach of stones, the introductory scene this time out sees Idle playing 'Jerusalem' (though referencing 'teeth') on a guitar, apparently at 'The Cardiff Rooms, Libya'. The first sketch proper has Cleese and Chapman as women in an art gallery swapping stories of their young children vandalising artworks, and finally eating them. This somewhat weak offering cuts back to Idle, still singing and playing though now being caressed by an attractive woman. The caption 'It's a man's life at the Cardiff Rooms, Libya' leads into Chapman's 'Colonel' character complaining about the plagiarism of the slogan 'It's a man's life in the modern army'. This is the start of a running joke of recurring 'It's a man's life...' slogans, all of which anger the colonel immensely.

16

A silent sketch follows with Terry Jones in the part of a man in straw boater and old-fashioned holiday clothes trying to get changed for the beach, with ever more improbable sets of circumstances leading to him being exposed with his trousers down. The sketch is very funny, though atypically 'Benny Hill' like for *Python*, and it is marred slightly by an overlong 'striptease' scene at the end.

This leads into the celebrated 'Fresh Fruit' sketch, with Cleese as a self-defence instructor training his reluctant pupils in ways to defend themselves against assailants with said fresh fruit, waving away Idle's appeals for him to teach them to defend themselves against a pointed stick. When these reluctant students play the part of attacking him, he disposes them by shooting the banana-wielding Chapman, then having been persuaded to abandon his gun, disposing of the raspberry-equipped Palin, Jones and Idle with, firstly, a 16-ton weight and then by releasing a tiger.

After a Gilliam animation link into a short sequence showing a king being carried by footmen to the beach in a sedan chair, getting out, undressing and then getting back in to be carried into the sea, the final sketch is a lengthy and somewhat convoluted one opening with Idle entering a bookshop in which Cleese refuses to sell him any books. A situation soon develops involving spy code phrases before the whole thing is revealed to be an elaborate web of counter-espionage involving fillings, teeth and the murderous reach of the feared British Dental Association. The episode ends with a football referee blowing a whistle and the 'It's' man climbing back up the cliff, from which he is immediately thrown again.

Comments.

The title of this episode, 'Owl Stretching Time', was one of the names originally considered as the title of the show.

Apart from Cleveland, who plays the nurse in the Dentists sketch, two other non-Pythons appear. Unusually, one of these, the writer and occasional actor Dick Vosburgh, has a credited speaking part in that same sketch. The sexy girl in the Cardiff Rooms, Libya is played by an uncredited Katya Wyeth, who appeared in a range of TV roles in the 1970s. She also appears briefly as the Art Critic's Wife, at the end of the Art Gallery sketch, and while she has a speaking part ('But it's my only line!'), she is nonetheless uncredited. Her 'Watteau, dear?' line, as she brings some water, is a pun referencing the 18th-century artist Antoine Watteau, and one which the studio audience, perhaps unsurprisingly, appear to entirely miss.

The 'Undressing In Public' sketch was filmed in Bournemouth. The crowds of people who can be seen watching in the beach scenes were actually curious passers-by, anxious to see what lunacy was going on.

The clip of the referee blowing his whistle was taken from the 1969 Scottish Cup Final, between Celtic and Rangers.

The 'Fresh Fruit' sketch has been referenced many times by other works, with one of the most unlikely being the children's book *The Slippery Slope* by Lemony Snickett, which contains the line 'If you don't give me a bunch of strawberries right now, I'm going to attack you with this large pointed stick'.

Author's Pick.
Generally, this episode has longer sketches than some others, with just short links in between and there is also less Gilliam animated footage. The final sketch, while containing some brilliant material, sags a little under its length, while the similarly excellent 'Undressing In Public' is spoilt slightly by an overlong conclusion. Owing to that, I would rate the 'Fresh Fruit' sketch as the pick of this episode.

Episode Five: Man's Crisis of Identity in the Latter Half of the Twentieth Century

First aired 16 November 1969
Sketches include:
Confuse-a-Cat
The Smuggler
A Duck, a Cat and a Lizard
Police Raid
Newsreader Arrested
Erotic Film
Silly Job Interview

Burglar

Synopsis:
After the long-suffering 'It's' man this time approaches in a rowing boat, we are taken to a quiet suburban home, to which a vet has been called to attend a cat which is 'moping'. The dramatic vet, played by Chapman, announces that the cat is in a rut, and must be confused, which brings in 'Confuse-A-Cat Ltd', who perform a series of bizarre stage routines for the bored feline, which eventually enters the house, cured. After this surreal opening, we cut to a customs desk where Cleese confronts a nervous-looking Palin, who is carrying a suitcase with a 'Zurich' sticker on it. He hopelessly denies having any Swiss timepieces in the case, claiming, against the 'Zurich' evidence to have come from Spain. He is then interrupted by the sound of an alarm clock from inside the case, followed by mass ticking and chiming. He admits he is a smuggler, only for Cleese to disbelieve him, despite the case being opened and found to be stuffed full of clocks.

Following this is a TV discussion about the moral implications of smuggling, although this loses its effectiveness when we find the three studio guests are a duck, a cat and a lizard. Several people in the street are asked their opinion, finishing with Idle who is playing chess in his house. A policeman(Chapman) enters and asks about 'illicit substances'. When this is denied he plants a brown paper bag very obviously, which is found to contain his sandwiches, giving way to another unusual *Python* punchline ('Blimey! Whatever did I give the wife?'), followed by more 'vox pop' interviews.

Two short scenes follow: the first has Idle as a newsreader with himself behind another desk on the screen behind him. He reports on a man being arrested, and we see himself on the screen being taken away and then released. The 'screen Idle' then announces a newsreader is to be arrested, and the main Idle is taken away. This is all very 'meta', as the term has it. Following this we see another sketch with a punchline as a couple named Dora and Bevis are seen intertwining sensually in their bedroom, despite being introduced as 'Match of the Day'. They fall on the bed, and we cut to clichéd scenes of rockets, trains into tunnels, volcanoes, then chimneys collapsing etc. Cut to Dora who asks him if he is just going to show films all night, as he sits at the foot of the bed with a projector.

A lengthy Gilliam animation sequence spoofing the old Charles Atlas 'sand in the face' advertisements leads into Cleese interviewing Chapman for a 'management training course'. He confuses the hapless applicant with a bizarre series of sounds and facial expressions before a panel of four judges enter to give Chapman marks out of ten for his own answers. The final sketch of this rather quickfire show has Idle ringing a doorbell and introducing himself as a burglar. A woman answers and accuses him of selling encyclopedias, to which he assures her that he is only planning to come in and steal a few things. She then lets him in and, predictably, he begins trying to sell her some encyclopedias.

Comments.

The title sequence of this episode is the first to feature Cleese announcing the title in a funny voice rather than a deadpan delivery.

Although the BBC had been broadcasting programmes in colour 'unofficially' for a while, 15 November 1969 was the date when they officially began colour programming. Therefore this episode, aired the following day, was the first to be advertised as 'broadcast in colour'.

The 'Confuse-A-Cat' sketch was filmed in an actual back garden, in Worcester Park, Surrey, on the same day as the Bicycle Repair Man sketch from Episode Three. The music accompanying the 'show' is called 'Action Station', by Dave Lindup. The crest on the 'Confuse-A-Cat' lorry appears to suggest that the company enjoy a seemingly unlikely Royal Charter. The full list of their incorporated companies credited at the end of the sketch is: Amaze-A-Vole Ltd, Stun-A-Stoat Ltd, Puzzle-A-Puma Ltd, Startle-A-Thompson's Gazelle Ltd, Bewilderbeest Inc and Distract-A-Bee.

Some of the 'Freudian' images during the Erotic Film sketch are borrowed from Hitchcock, who used the tunnel, fireworks etc. himself, notably in *North*

By Northwest. The image of the refuelling plane is a nod to the title sequence of Kubrick's *Dr Strangelove*, while the baffling inclusion of Richard Nixon appears to be merely part of the regular referencing of him in the show. During the sketch, the newsreader reappears in shot to confirm that this is, indeed, not 'Match Of The Day', and informs us that on BBC2 Joan Bakewell will be talking to Michael Dean. Bakewell and Dean were presenters on the programme *Late Night Line-Up*.

During the 'vox pop' comments, the appearance of Carol Cleveland as a woman opining that 'asking Margaret Drabble' (the well-known novelist) would be an alternative to a lizard, is the first instance of a female character having a funny line which is not part of a 'sexy female' shot.

Author Picks.
This is a somewhat hit-and-miss episode, with some scenes suffering from sagging pacing ('Confuse-A-Cat' for instance contains a hopelessly overlong scene of the show performed for the cat). 'The Smuggler', Erotic Film' and 'Burglar' are all very strong, but the 'Silly Job Interview' may win out if only for the classic Cleese performances. Foreshadowing some of his other tour-de-force performance such as 'The Ministry Of Silly Walks', it is fair to say that no other comedian in the world could have made this one work as well as it does.

Episode Six: It's The Arts
First Aired 23 November 1969
Sketches include:
Johann Gambolputty
Non-illegal Robbery
Crunchy Frog
The Dull Life of a City Stockbroker
Red Indian in Theatre
A Scotsman on a Horse
Twentieth-Century Vole

Synopsis:
The 'It's' man opens this episode by running, in speeded-up fashion, to answer a phone in the middle of nowhere – which seems odd, but there is a payoff to come. The first sketch proper sees a series of joke captions, mainly about the price of the captions, before Chapman is seen presenting a fictional show 'It's The Arts', in which the topic is the little known composer Johann Gambolputty de von Ausfern-schplenden-schlitter-crasscrenbon-fried-digger-dingle-dangle-dongle-dungle-burstein-von-knacker-thrasher-apple-banger-horowitz-ticolensic-grander-knotty-spelltinkle-grandlich-grumblemeyer-spelterwasser-kurstlich-himbleeisen-bahnwagen-gutenabend-bitte-ein-nurnburger-bratwustle-gernspurten-mitz-weimache-luber-hundsfut-gumberaber-shonedanker-kalbsfleisch-mittler-aucher von Hautkopft of Ulm. The rather weak sketch

revolves around constant repetition of this full name, and an aged interviewee dying before the question is asked. Next up is a gang of desperate-sounding criminals who, to the consternation of one of their number, never break the law. They are planning an elaborate raid to buy a watch. After some more 'vox pops', we join the police entering the premises of the Whizzo confectionery company (reusing the Whizzo Butter name from Episode One). Learning of the contents of such favours as Crunchy Frog, Ram's Bladder Cup, Anthrax Ripple and Cockroach Cluster, the chocolates are confiscated after the Spring Surprise turn out to puncture the cheeks with two large bolts when eaten.

A silent routine follows, entitled 'The Dull Life Of A City Stockbroker', in which we see Palin in the title role heading to work, complete with bowler hat, umbrella and briefcase. Along his journey, by foot, bus and taxi, scenes of sex, violence, death and high adventure play out constantly just behind him. When he reaches the office, he sits down seemingly oblivious to the woman with a knife in her back, feet dangling from the ceiling and a writhing couple on his desk, and he begins reading a comic entitled *Thrills And Adventure*. Following this, we enter a theatre, with a genteel crowd, among whom sits Idle as a wildly stereotypical Red Indian, complete with war paint and bow and arrows, announcing he is 'heap big fan of Cicely Courtneidge'. We learn that his tribe often visit Leatherhead Rep, as the stage manager Stan Wilson is 'heap big friend'. When it is announced that Cicely Courtneidge is unable to appear, the announcer is shot with arrows.

After an appeal to have a policeman as a pen-pal, the next item is introduced as 'A Scotsman on a Horse'. This was also introduced in Episode One after the nine-legged man runs away, but this time we see Cleese riding furiously across the Scottish landscape to stop a wedding which is going ahead in a small church. He arrives in the nick of time, storms down the aisle and carries away the groom. Finally, we enter the offices of film company 20th Century Vole, where producer Larry Salzberg throws a series of utterly stupid ideas at a crew of writers, all of whom are too terrified to disagree. Finally, he picks up the phone, which rings next to the 'It's' man again, who answers. The credits roll, and, they list Larry Salzberg as having done everything in the episode, except the cast who all have 'Berg' added to their names.

Comments.

The captions at the beginning include 'The BBC Entry to the Zinc Stoat of Budapest'. This references the comedy award, *The Golden Rose Of Montreux*, which *Python* would enter, unsuccessfully, in 1971 with a compilation episode.

The full name in the Johann Gambolputty sketch takes twenty seconds to say. It is repeated five times in full.

During the City Stockbroker sketch, he is served in a newsagent by a topless woman, to which he seems oblivious. This is the only time *Python* ever used blatant nudity, and it is amazing that they got away with the gratuitousness of it pre-1970. We must assume that Carol Cleveland did not want to do this, as the woman is played by an uncredited Sheila Sands, who appeared in several quite small TV and film roles up until 1972, including the horror film *Virgin Witch*. She will crop up again in Episode eleven. The scene was edited out when the episode aired on American television.

The Theatre sketch appears to be filmed in the actual studio audience of the *Python* recording. The woman sitting on the other side of Idle from Chapman is reportedly named Constance Carling.

Ian Davidson again appears in this episode, as one of the 20th Century Vole writers.

Dame Cicely Courtneidge, who is the Red Indian's favourite, was a celebrated actress who passed away in 1987 aged 97. She played the part of Stan's mum in the first series of *On The Buses*. His chief's favourites, Michael Denison and Dulcie Gray, were respected husband-and-wife actors who were married for 59 years.

The 16 Ton Weight from the Fresh Fruit sketch makes another appearance here, albeit in animated form. Another appearance of the man-eating pram from Episode Two sees the pram cornered by a police searchlight, where the pram, carnivorous baby and all, are squashed under the unexpectedly dropped weight.

The Whizzo Chocolates received a tip of the hat by JK Rowling decades later, when the Harry Potter characters eat a variety of chocolate called Cockroach Cluster.

Author's Pick.
Not the finest episode, several of the sketches in this show don't really work quite as well as they should, with Johann Gambolputty, in particular, growing tedious quickly. The Theatre sketch and the law-abiding robbers are, however, excellent, but the highlight here is probably the Crunchy Frog scene, if only for its lasting impact.

Episode Seven: You're No Fun Any More
First Aired 30 November 1969
Sketches include:
Camel Spotting
The Audit
Science Fiction Sketch

Synopsis:
Unusually, over half of this episode revolves around one extended sketch, the 'Science Fiction Sketch'. Prior to that, however, there are a few lesser routines strung together. The 'It's' man gets us underway, arriving through dense undergrowth before forgetting his line and having to be prompted. 'Camel Sketch' is the first offering, with Idle portraying the titular Camel Spotter, who has failed to spot a single one in several years, a record as poor as when

he was a 'Yeti Spotter'. It turns out that he is actually a trainspotter when he announces that the difference between a dromedary and a camel is that 'a dromedary has one hump and a camel has a refreshment car, buffet, and ticket collector'. When called out on this, he says 'you're no fun any more', leading into people using that line in unlikely situations. The following sketch has Palin as an accountant in a board meeting being fund out having embezzled a penny, leading to a somewhat incongruous bishop who is present using the 'no fun' line again and being tied to a railway line by Idle - having threatened to throw him 'under a camel'.

This opening has been uninspired so far. However, from the moment Palin's cheesy presenter introduces the 'Science Fiction Sketch' things take a turn for the better. The lengthy and rambling routine concerns the mystery of Englishmen being turned into Scotsmen by a flying saucer beam and rushing north of the border. This is finally discovered to be an alien threat when a small Scottish family kilt-making business receives an order for 48 million kilts from the planet Skyron in the Andromeda galaxy. The order was also, oddly, placed by a giant blancmange, which promptly eats the kilt-maker's wife. It turns out that this is all part of a dastardly plot for the aliens to win Wimbledon by only having the world's worst tennis-playing nation to beat. Sadly, this plan fails when the blancmange in the Wimbledon final is eaten by Mr & Mrs Brainsample, who are themselves, aliens. The punchline of a Scotsman winning Wimbledon by playing against himself seems odd now that Andy Murray - from Scotland himself - has done so well.

Comments.

Once again there is no appearance from Carol Cleveland. The sizeable part of the glamorous laboratory assistant in the Science Fiction Sketch, along with a that of a woman who declares Dracula to be 'No fun anymore' when his fangs fall out, is played by Donna Reading, who was quite a regular on TV screens in largely minor roles between the mid-'60s and the mid-'70s.

After the Embezzlement sketch, two captions explaining where to write in order to complain are shown, both with entirely different voice-overs. The first of these reads 'MR ALBERT SPIM, I,OOO,OO8 LONDON ROAD, OXFORD' but is accompanied by Cleese saying 'The Royal Frog Trampling Institute, 16 Rayners Lane, London, W.C. Fields', while the second reads 'FLIGHT LT. & PREBENDARY ETHEL MORRIS, THE DIMPLES, THAXTED, NR BUENOS AIRES', but is read aloud as 'Tristram and Isolde Phillips, 7.30 Covent Garden Saturday, near Sunday, and afterwards at the Inigo Jones Fish Emporium'.

The tennis scenes were shot at the Lammas Park Tennis Club, Ealing, quite near to Wimbledon. The football stadium with just one player and one fan is supposed to be Brentford FC, which is near to the studios in Ealing – although it looks quite different from how it does today. The player is not wearing Brentford's kit, however, and the colours appear to most closely represent Scottish club Motherwell.

The location in the Science Fiction sketch is shown as being New Pudsey: there is no such place, though there is a Pudsey in Yorkshire.

The Audit sketch reminds us of just how long ago these episodes were filmed when the firm is announced to have made a profit of 'one shilling' (one-twentieth of a pound in old pre-decimal British currency).

There is a smaller amount of Gilliam animation in this episode than any other thus far.

Author's Pick.

In this episode, there is really no contest. The opening sketches are generally weak fare, but the whole of the lengthy 'Science Fiction Sketch' is a triumph, which is perhaps surprising given that it is the team's first attempt at a lengthy, structured narrative, and as such could be expected to be a little more formative.

Episode Eight: Full Frontal Nudity.

First Aired 7 December 1969
Sketches include:
Army Protection Racket
Art Critic – The Place of the Nude
Buying a Bed
Hermits
Dead Parrot sketch
The Flasher
Hell's Grannies

Synopsis:

The 'It's' man appears to be having it easy this time out, as we find him being plied with wine by an attractive woman. Just as he utters his word, however, she hands him a large bomb. With 'BOMB' written on it. A caption shows the episode title as 'Full Frontal Nudity', and we begin with some more of those 'vox pops' on that very subject before we enter an Army colonel's office (Chapman). A private (Idle) enters and explains that he wishes to leave the army (after one day) because it is 'dangerous'. While they argue about this, two Italian mobsters are shown in and proceed to attempt to extort protection money for not breaking any tanks or indeed any of the men. After a short while, Chapman calls a halt to this because it is 'silly', and also as the commanding officer he has not had any funny lines. Many of the sketches in this episode are halted by the colonel in this way.

After some more 'vox pops' and a Gilliam animation featuring a 'Full Frontal Nudity' show in which the frontals in question are obscured in ever more absurd ways, we return to the art critic from Episode Four, to discuss the role of nudity. His wife enters, delivers a terrible joke and, as with that previous episode, follows it up with 'But it's my only line!' We cut to a country scene as the announcer says we will leave the critic to strangle his wife, but after a short while, we come across him strangling her in the foreground of the shot.

We then see a man carrying his bride across country, through streets and into a bed shop, where we find two salesmen, one of whom exaggerates all of his numbers by a factor of ten, while the other reduces his by three quarters. After this confusion, the husband and wife customers are directed to a third salesman (Chapman) to buy a mattress but are informed that they must ask for a dog kennel because if anyone says the word 'mattress' to him, he will put a paper bag on his head. They do, and he does, whereupon the other two salesmen have to climb into a tea chest and sing 'Jerusalem' until he stops. This happens twice before the salesman in question insists that he is fine with the word mattress. The wife (Cleveland, who returns this week) then says the word, and when the paper bag returns, and she is berated, she appeals again 'But it's my only line!'

The colonel then stops things again, demands some fresh air and we go to another sketch in which two hermits (Palin and Idle) meet on a hill and discuss their caves. They meet other hermits, who it turns out lodge with each other in shared caves and generally get along as a community. After the line that 'one thing about a hermit, at least you meet people', the Colonel stops proceedings again and the cast is swept off the hillside in an animation sequence which sees them fed into a sausage grinder and coming out in the form of a dancing Botticelli Venus. From there we are directed into none other than 'the Dead Parrot Sketch'. This is a sketch so familiar, that most of the western world appears to know it by heart. This original version differs from later ones on stage and in the *And Now For Something Completely Different* film by not leading into the 'Lumberjack Song'. Instead, after some confusion as regards whether they are in Bolton or Ipswich when Cleese asks for a replacement parrot, the Colonel again stops proceedings.

The next short routine shows a man opening a grubby raincoat to flash passers-by before he eventually turns to us and we see he is fully clothed with a sign saying 'Boo!' This leads into 'Hell's Grannies', in which a neighbourhood is terrorised by marauding gangs of violent old ladies. The Colonel allows this to proceed until a vicar is bullied by 'a vicious gang of Keep Left signs', whereupon he stops it again. The 'It's' man then reappears, manages to put out the fuse on his bomb, runs away at high speed and is predictably blown up.

Comments.
Carol Cleveland is in this episode again, playing the wife in the bed shop, but several other women also play parts in the show. The two credited are Katya Wyeth, reprising her role as the art critic's wife, and Rita Taylor, who plays the wife of the man abducted by the 'baby snatchers' in the Hell's Grannies sketch. Uncredited are Donna Reading, who plays the girl with the 'It's' man and Swedish actress Ewa Aulin as a young woman harassed by the Grannies.

When we see the Hell's Grannies painting 'Make Tea Not War' onto a wall, we are told it is in Bolton, but the existing graffiti about Queen's Park Rangers football club identifies it clearly as London. In fact, the scene was shot in Australia Road, East Acton, very near to BBC Television Centre.

The 'Dead Parrot Sketch' has been referenced countless times in popular culture, but surely one of its most unusual namechecks came when Margaret Thatcher referenced it when talking about the Liberal Democrats and their dove symbol! She also closed her speech by saying 'And now for something completely different'.

Conversely, there were several similar precursors to the sketch. In 1959, Tony Hancock did a similar routine involving a dead tortoise, in 1963 Benny Hill did a sketch in which a taxidermist attempts to pass a stuffed duck off as a parrot, and throughout the '60s the comedian Freddie 'Parrot-face' Davies would routinely carry a dead parrot around in a cage, often complaining about the man who sold it to him. By far the earliest of these, however, dates back to 400BC when the Greek playwrights Hierocles and Philagrius wrote a comic routine in which a man complains to a merchant that his newly aquired slave is dead.

Two of the salesmen in the bed shop are named Mr Verity and Mr Lambert. This is a nod to Verity Lambert, the first Producer of *Dr Who*, among other things. Name tags were intended for these characters, but not used.

Author's Pick.
The obvious thing here would be to single out the 'Dead Parrot' sketch, but I will refrain from doing so, partly because over-familiarity has dulled it slightly, but also because the sketch became snappier and sharper in future performances on stage and film. Instead, I will plump (pun entirely intended) for the mattress selling, if only for it's sheer absurdity.

Episode Nine: The Ant, An Introduction
First Aired 14 December 1969
Sketches include:
Llamas
Kilimanjaro Expedition
Homicidal Barber
The Lumberjack Song
The Refreshment Room at Bletchley
Hunting Film
The Visitors

Synopsis:
The 'It's' man runs to the foreground dodging gunfire, as we are taken to the first item, which has Cleese as a manically voiced Mexican announcer together with Idle and Jones as a guitarist and dancer. Cleese delivers an absurd lecture about Llamas, including the facts that they are equipped with fins for swimming and large beaks for eating honey. We then cut, via Cleese at a desk behind a cafe saying 'And now for something completely different', to a short segment of a man

with a tape recorder up his nose, which he plays and rewinds with a dramatically flourished finger. We cut to an office where a man named Arthur (Idle) is applying to join a mountaineering party up Kilimanjaro, only to find that the man interviewing him (Sir George Head – Cleese) has double vision and believes there are two peaks. It becomes clear that nobody in the party even knows what a mountaineer is, and when Chapman enters as the supposed party leader and climbs all over the furniture, Arthur leaves, and we see the joke revealed that one Arthur is left and two Cleeses are talking to him.

A man with a tape recorder up his brother's nose takes us to a barbershop, where the barber concerned (Palin) has enormous difficulty preventing his seemingly rogue homicidal hand from stabbing his customer (Jones – who seems unconcerned that the barber's jacket is covered with blood). After some close shaves (pun, of course, intended), including setting a tape recorder running behind Jones while he hides, he reveals that he really wanted to be a lumberjack, and we are into the famous 'Lumberjack Song', which is almost as well known as the 'Dead Parrot Sketch'. Connie Booth, then Cleese's wife, plays his girl in the song. Two short routines follow, with a terrible joke which we are told has been submitted as the UK entry for 'The Rubber Mac Of Zurich Award', and finished last, and a Gumby crooning while hitting himself on the head with bricks. Idle then plays his usual sleazy compère, announcing an act with such obsequious toadying that he drops to the floor writhing. The act does not turn up, so we are treated to a man with inflatable knees and a very overlong animated sequence of dancers.

Next up, a silent film of upper-class men hunting with increasing ineptitude (seeming to presage the later 'Upper-Class Twit Of The Year' competition), is followed by Cleese announcing the final sketch from inside a henhouse, as the unrequired knight with the chicken trudges past. This final sketch has Chapman and Cleveland as a courting couple whose house is invaded by first Idle as Arthur Name, from his 'Nudge Nudge' sketch, who has invited himself after meeting Chapman in the pub some years previously. A string of ever more undesirable guests then arrive, including Cleese as the abhorrent Mr Equator, Gilliam as a recently bereaved man who is clad only in sequins, underpants, white wellington boots and a necklace, and Palin who enters with an incontinent goat. Cleveland runs from the room while Chapman, protesting, is shot by Mr Equator. A party of miners arrive, and they close with a sing-song at the piano.

Comments:

A far from vintage episode, this is nonetheless notable for two firsts: the first appearance of a Gumby (the men with knotted handkerchiefs on their heads and rolled up trousers) and also the first use of the famous 'And now for something completely different' line

In the 'Lumberjack Song', other than Cleese and Chapman, most of the chorus is comprised of the Fred Tomlinson Singers, who also appear as the singing miners in the final sketch. The song was released as a single in the UK in 1975, produced and mixed by *Python* fan George Harrison. This original sketch marks the first *Python* appearance for Connie Booth, later to become most famous for *Fawlty Towers*.

In the 'Homicidal Barber' sketch, when discussing the football, 'Hurst played well' is a football term and refers to Geoff Hurst, scorer of the 1966 World Cup Final hat trick, who played for West Ham United at the time. 'I prefer to watch Palace nowadays' is, of course, a reference to South London team Crystal Palace.

The 'Kilimanjaro Expedition' sketch has been compared to a scene in the Franz Kafka novel *The Castle*, a comic episode in which the protagonist is confused by twins who are assigned to assist him.

The 'Rubber Mac Of Zurich Award' is, of course, another reference to 'The Golden Rose Of Montreux'.

'The Lumberjack Song' has been sung in various snippets in a great number of TV programmes and films, but two of the most unexpected performances turned up in the Fantasy computer game *Baldur's Gate* and a 1984 episode of *The A Team*.

Author's Pick.
A textbook example of the inconsistency of some *Python* work, moments of genius here (Cleese in hen house, some of the llama lecture and Idle's club compère), are interspersed with long stretches which fall somewhat flat (the Kilimanjaro sketch, the animated dancers and the final 'Visitors' sketch in particular). The two best sketches in this episode are probably the barber and the hunting film, but I will give it to the 'Homicidal Barber', because of Palin's hilarious portrayal and the fact that it segues into the over-familiar but still iconic 'Lumberjack Song'.

Episode Ten: Untitled
First Aired 21 December 1969
Sketches include:
Bank Robber in a Lingerie Shop
It's A Tree
Vocational Guidance Counsellor
Ron Obvious
Pet Conversions
Gorilla Librarian
Letters to Daily Mirror
Strangers in the Night

Synopsis:
The 'It's' man is having a hard time of it this week, as we find him hung on a meat hook alongside a large number of ex-pigs. The first sketch shows a bank robber (Cleese) who mistakenly targets a lingerie shop to rob at gunpoint. There is also a rather surreal introduction with Palin as a plumber receiving

a letter from the BBC asking him to do a walk-on part. The following item depicts a chat show called 'It's A Tree', which is quite literal in that it is hosted by Arthur Tree who is, in fact, a tree. The guests we see are a block of wood and a sheet of laminated plastic.

Moving on from this, we have the celebrated 'Vocational Guidance Counsellor' sketch, in which we see Cleese as the counsellor with Palin as Mr Anchovy, a chartered accountant who wants to be a lion tamer. This is despite Cleese's assurances that the ideal job for him has been found to be the one he already does, owing to the fact that he is, in fact, spectacularly dull and tedious. He will not be dissuaded from his chosen change of profession – until, that is, it is pointed out to him that the lions he has seen at the zoo eating ants were, in fact, anteaters. Unnerved by a real lion, Anchovy reverts to indecisive type.

From here we head to the exciting world of daredevil Ron Obvious (Jones), who is attempting to jump the channel. Having managed only around six feet as opposed to the 26 miles required, and hampered by the 56-pound bag of sponsor-provided bricks he is carrying, Obvious turns his attention to new heroic pursuits, each organised by his unscrupulous manager Luigi Vercotti. After injuring his jaw attempting to eat Chichester Cathedral, he fails to tunnel solo from Godalming to Java without a shovel, badly injures himself in a bid to split a railway carriage with his nose before perishing in an attempt to run to the planet Mercury.

Next we find ourselves in a pet shop with, like the 'Dead Parrot Sketch', Cleese and Palin facing off. Cleese wants to buy a cat, but Palin has only a terrier. After suggesting surgically altering the hapless animal to resemble a cat or a parrot, it is agreed to turn the terrier into a fish. This leads us to a gorilla being interviewed for the job of librarian. The twist is that when he is revealed as a librarian in a suit trying to get employment, it turns out that the Board only employ wild animals in librarian positions. After some strongly worded letters to the Daily Mirror, we find a couple (Jones and Palin) in bed asleep. Jones (the wife) begins to receive a string of suitors to her bedside, beginning with Idle as a bread-wielding Frenchman named Maurice, followed by Roger (Cleese), Biggles (Chapman) together with Algy in full flying gear, and finally a band of Mexican musicians called The Herman Rodrigues Four. After repeatedly waking up to be assured it is a trick of the light or branch against the window, Palin gets up to go to the toilet, just as a huge man enters dressed as an Aztec God. We cut to the bathroom where Palin is with a busty blonde, saying he fears his wife will be suspecting something. We close with a comment about a predictable ending cutting to a hilariously unpredictable animated sequence of very unlikely animals eating other animals and return to the 'It's' man being taken down from his hook.

Comments.
This is the first episode, and indeed the only one in this first series, to have no title displayed at the End Credits, and so is 'untitled'.

The 'Vocational Guidance Counsellor' was so influential in popularising the stereotype of accountancy being boring that, four decades later, the *Financial Times* ran a story regarding how this still haunts the profession.

In the 'Strangers In The Night' sketch, Herman Rodrigues is played by the writer and comedian Barry Cryer, Algy is another appearance by Ian Davidson, while the mistress in the bathroom is played by Carole Donoghue, who had only one more part after this when, in 1973, she reappeared from nowhere to appear in the film *Holiday On The Buses*.

Note that 'The Larch' from Episode Three makes a re-appearance here, in the 'Vocational Guidance Counsellor' sketch.

During the bank robbery in the lingerie shop, Cleese admonished himself by saying 'Adopt, adapt and improve. Motto of the Round Table'. This is, perhaps surprisingly, true, as the slogan of the Round Table organisation, which is written on much of their official documentation, is indeed 'adopt, adapt, improve'.

The scene of Ron Obvious attempting to eat Chichester Cathedral was actually filmed at Holy Trinity Church, Chertsey, Surrey. The beach scenes for the channel jump were mostly shot in Covehithe, Suffolk.

Author's Pick.
A hard choice here, as this is indeed a very strong episode. The 'Strangers In The Night' sketch is very funny, as is the 'Gorilla Librarian', and either could have been the highlight of a weaker show. However, the award has to go to the quite brilliant 'Vocational Guidance Counsellor', for both its performances and its lasting influence.

Episode Eleven: The Royal Philharmonic Orchestra Goes to the Bathroom
First Aired 28 December 1969
Sketches include:
Lavatorial Humour
Interruptions
Agatha Christie Sketch
Literary Football Discussion
Interesting People
Undertakers Film
Eighteenth-Century Social Legislation
The Battle of Trafalgar
Batley Townswomen's Guild Presents the Battle of Pearl Harbour

Synopsis:
Another rather unsatisfactory episode, and indeed one heavily criticised my Michael Palin himself in his published diaries. Nevertheless, it does have its

moments. The 'It's' man opens things by walking across a road toward the camera. He gets hit by four cars, but stays on his feet until he reaches the pavement, says his word and is immediately run over by a woman with a pram. The first sketch is nothing more than a quick gag giving the episode its title, as Palin knocks on a bathroom door asking if the occupants are finished yet, to be met by a blast of Tchaikovsky's 'Piano Concerto Number One' from inside. Several 'viewers' letters bemoaning the content already lead us into a programme called 'The World Of History' introduced by Chapman who is constantly interrupted by clips of undertakers whenever he mentions anything historically about death. A film of two hearses racing on a country road and crashing near a sign reading 'Accident Black Spot' with the same undertakers picnicking beneath it infuriates him so much that he walks off.

We move next to a drawing room with an Agatha Christie feel to it, as Cleese as Inspector Tiger is telling nobody to leave as there has been a murder, but he keeps getting his words wrong. Eventually, two surgeons rush in and lobotomise him with a large saw, and he appears to improve. The lights go out, a gunshot is heard, and when they come back on the Inspector is slumped dead with an arrow through his head holding a large bottle of poison. Several other policemen enter and end up dead in a similar fashion. The sketch is cut short for a 'literary football discussion', in which Idle's highbrow philosophical discussion of the match between Jarrow and Bologna leaves the - clearly extremely stupid - guest footballer Jimmy Buzzard (Cleese), nonplussed. This sketch is again cut short as we return to the drawing-room where there is now an enormous pile of dead policeman, as another is shot and a caption reads 'Constables 13, Superintendents 9'.

Another short undertaker comic clip takes us to Idle, as a man interviewing 'Interesting People' for another show. These people include: a man half an inch tall inside a matchbox, a madman, a bicycle bell choir performing 'Men Of Harlech', a human stapler who can give cats influenza, an invisible man who, it turns out, is merely so tedious he is ignored by everyone, and finally a man claiming to be able to recite the entire bible in one second while being struck over the head with a large axe. He actually manages only the first two words before his demise. A break for 'Interesting Sport', featuring 'all-in cricketing', in a wrestling ring, leads us to a man from Dorchester who loves shouting, a man who can fling a cat into a bucket of water, and a man who can hypnotise bricks.

The 'Undertakers' running routine now concludes with the tired undertakers climbing into the coffin, which moves on its own at high speed to the graveside. The gravediggers are motioned out, and eight of them appear, followed by two miners with lamps, two convicts, a policeman with dog and an Australian with a surfboard. The 'History' theme is back next, purporting to examine 18th Century social legislation but instead merely showing film of extremely sexy women and strippers. Chapman's professor returns, and we see some 'Gumby' figures claiming that the Battle Of Trafalgar was, in fact, fought near Cudworth in South Yorkshire, and also that cement is interesting.

The show is concluded by the spectacle of the Batley Townswomen's Guild presenting their re-enactment of the Battle of Pearl Harbour, which actually turns out to consist of them fighting each other with handbags in a muddy field. Finally, it is back to the 'It's' man, who walks back carefully across the road untroubled by any traffic until he gets knocked into a hedge by the pram again.

Comments.

This is an episode that Palin was very critical of. He described it in his diaries as 'painfully slow', and that good ideas such as the 'History' and 'Undertakers' sketches had their life drained by weak editing, shooting and performance.

The bicycle bell choir in the 'Interesting People' sketch is, in fact, interesting. They are named the Rachel Toovey Bicycle Choir, and Rachel Toovey is a real person – indeed a renowned Australian physiotherapist who works in celebrated fashion with bicycle therapy for disabled children. However, she would not have been born until over a decade after the show aired, which raises the fascinating prospect of this either being a) a startling coincidence or b) Ms Toovey deciding upon her much-lauded career and research, based upon an old *Python* sketch! Either way, it certainly counts as 'interesting'...

This episode marks the first appearance of multiple 'Gumbys', although they are not yet filmed together.

The reference to (and film of) 'Mary Bignal's wonderful jump in 1964' in one of the letters at the beginning of the episode actually refers to the British athlete Mary Rand. Her maiden name was Bignal, though by the time she set a world record with that famous jump she had already been married to rower Sid Rand for three years and was already known as Rand, so the reason for the use of her maiden name is unclear. However, around the time of this episode's airing, in December 1969, she married again, to American decathlete Bill Toomey, so that may have some bearing.

Carol Cleveland plays the two main female roles in this episode, Lady Velloper in the 'Agatha Christie' sketch and the sexy woman in the second 'History' sketch. The other female parts are Maureen Flanagan (again), playing Anona Winn in the 'Christie' sketch and an uncredited appearance by Sheila Sands (the 'topless newsagent' of Episode Six) as the stripper in the second 'History' sketch. Ian Davidson appears again, as one of the 'lobotomy surgeons' and Chief Constable Fire, both in the Christie sketch.

Cleese's footballer Jimmy Buzzard is taken from his 'fictional forward line' of 'Bun, Wackett, Buzzard, Stubble and Boot', which was one of the touted names for the show.

Author's Pick.

This is a difficult one because, as correctly noted by Palin, the episode abounds with good ideas not executed well enough. The running 'Undertakers' sketch is probably the strongest thread in the episode, so takes the honours, though 'Interesting People' is a close second.

Episode Twelve: The Naked Ant

First Aired 4 January 1970
Sketches include:
Falling From Building
Spectrum – Talking About Things
Mr Hilter and the Minehead By-election
Silly Voices at the Police station
Upper-Class Twit of the Year
Ken Shabby
How Far Can a Minister Fall?

Synopsis:

The 'It's' man is in a pinball machine this time out – we see the ball being fired before he bounces to the foreground from tree to tree. Following a brief, and bizarre, scene of a railway signalman wrestling with a bear in the signal box, we cut to an office where Idle and Cleese see several men fall past the window. They deduce it to be a board meeting and bet on the next man to fall. This leads into a spoof TV show called 'Spectrum' which lampoons the sort of breathless political programmes brilliantly, with Palin's 100mph host a joy.

After an animated sequence, again dealing with falling people, we are into a real classic of early *Python*, as an extremely boring couple from Coventry arrive at a Minehead guest house, talking tediously about the journey. In the dining room, they are introduced to three other guests, Mr Hilter, Ron Vibbentrop and Mr Bimmler, who are of course the three high-ranking Nazis in very thin disguise. Hitler and Himmler are still in their uniforms, while Von Ribbentrop for some reason has a top hat. They are contesting the local election under the slogan 'Hilter – for a better Meinhead'.

The next sketch sees a rather unnecessary sequence at a police station where each of the policemen can only understand speech at a certain volume and pitch. It gets irritating rather quickly, but no matter, as the legendary 'Upper-Class Twit Of The Year' is along next, with the five main Pythons (and Cleese's commentary) combining to make this pseudo-athletic event a work of genius. The upper-class feel is retained in the following 'Ken Shabby' sketch, in which the very posh Chapman is speaking to Palin's revolting Ken Shabby about his engagement to his daughter (Connie Booth). This is followed by an inspired animated sequence in which Jones discards his pipe in distaste, and when it drops, a procession of creatures crawl out of it. These include what seems to be a penguin, a vole, a flea, a grasshopper and a blue whale.

We are back to the political programming next, where a minister for the 'Wood Party' is delivering a Party Political Broadcast when he unexpectedly falls through the Earth's crust. A rope is lowered while he attempts to continue with his broadcast, dangling upside down in a deep cavern. Palin returns as the motormouth presenter, cutting quickly to several outside guests with little to say, including the railwayman with the bear again. We return to 'Pinball It's' and close...

Comments.

The 'Mr Hilter' sketch was the subject of some confusion over one particular line, which was incorrectly transcribed for decades. When Mr McGoebbels phones for Hilter, the latter says 'If he opens his big mouth again, it's lampshade time!' Anyone looking up the line for clarification would most likely have found 'It's Lapschig time!' as the official wording. Many people spent fruitless hours attempting to find a translation of this German word – fruitlessly as it happens, as it doesn't exist. The correct wording IS 'lampshade', which was only confirmed by the original scripts much later as the 'official' script copies contained the error. The 'lampshade' joke is, in fact, very dark, and extremely daring for the time, as it refers to the story – since claimed to be false, or at least without any confirmation – of the Buchenwald Camp Commandant having a lampshade made from human skin, from inmates. One wonders whether the supposed 'Lapschig' mistake was purposefully done to divert any controversy from this darkest of satire.

The 'Upper-Class Twit Of The Year' competition was filmed at Hurlingham Park, Fulham, which is a multi-use sports complex, mainly for rugby and football, and is the home of Hammersmith And Fulham Rugby Club.

Carol Cleveland does not appear in this episode. Connie Booth plays Ken Shabby's 'intended', Rosamund, while Flanagan, once again, appears in non-speaking roles as Mrs Johnson, the wife of the boring man from Coventry, and a 'lovely girl', who gives an opinion in a dubbed male voice. There are other young women, such as in the 'Upper-Class Twit' sketch who are unidentified.

When first broadcast in Finland, the 'Upper-Class Twit Of The Year Show' was somehow interpreted as mocking people with cerebral palsy, and Finnish TV stopped broadcasting the show immediately!

The foot does not come down at the end of the credits of this episode, though this may possibly be merely an editing error. But knowing *Python*, who knows?

Author's Pick.

This very strong episode has several sketches which could be standouts in a weaker show. However, there is, for me, a clear shortlist of two: 'Mr Hilter' and 'Upper-Class Twit'. Both are brilliant, but if only for the reason that the definitive version of 'Upper-Class Twit' may well be the one in the *And Now For Something Completely Different* film, I will plump for Mr Hilter and his chums. Some of the attention to detail in that sketch is magnificent.

Episode Thirteen: Intermission
First Aired 11 January 1970
Sketches include:
Restaurant Cannibalism
Advertisements
Albatross
Me Doctor

Historical Impersonations
Probe-Around on Crime
Mr. Attila the Hun
Psychiatry / Operating Theatre

Synopsis:
The undertakers reappear at the beginning of the episode, with the lid opening to reveal the 'It's' man. After a short 'intermission' (the running gag this time out), the first sketch sees Cleese and Idle as a couple arriving at a restaurant which keeps assuring them strongly that it is entirely vegetarian. After a while it begins to dawn that it is, in fact, cannibalistic, a theory supported by a semi-naked Terry Jones as 'Hopkins' being wheeled in sitting on a larger serving dish with an apple in his mouth (or is it a tomato?). Some of Cleese's dialogue referring to his constantly complaining wife ('Please excuse my wife. She may appear to be rather nasty, but underneath she has a heart of Formica') could come straight from the lips of Basil Fawlty.

Another intermission brings us cinema advertisements familiar to cinema-goers of the '60s and '70s in the UK, first for a local car dealership (located 'on the second floor') and then for a restaurant, which is clearly being raided for pornography as the cameras roll. The cinema theme is continued with the 'Albatross' sketch, with Cleese as ice-cream seller shouting that he has albatross for sale, carrying a tray with one huge such sea-bird on it. Jones is a customer who, disappointed that it's only sea-bird flavour and doesn't come with wafers, nevertheless buys one.

Two of the weaker, albeit short, sequences follow, with Cleese as a policeman who has a robbery reported to him before being asked by the complainant to 'come back to my place'. He agrees and there lies the joke, such as it is. Then we have a short hospital scene revolving around confusion to do with the phrases 'Me, doctor?' 'No, me doctor, you patient'. It's essentially the Abbott And Costello 'Who's On First' routine in new trousers. Thankfully, things get right back on track with smarmy TV host Palin introducing 'Historical Impersonations', which include Cardinal Richelieu doing Petula Clark, Julius Caesar doing Eddie Waring, Florence Nightingale doing Brian London (essentially getting hit with a boxing glove), Ivan The Terrible as a sales assistant from Freeman Hardy Willis and Napoleon as The R101 Disaster. Finally, a Gumby requests John The Baptist doing an impersonation of Graham Hill, which is basically a severed head with a moustache driving at speed. The final impersonation is Marcel Marceau as a man getting a 16 Ton Weight dropped on his head, which ends as one might expect.

A fairly lengthy routine follows regarding the police using magic and the occult to solve crime, covering magic wands, Ouija boards and sacrifices at Stonehenge. This leads directly into another police sketch finding Attila The Hun turn up at the station, though he is actually a timid man in glasses (Palin), who was named Attila The by his parents, Mr And Mrs Norman Hun. He turns himself in for pillaging and looting a city, but a breathalyser reveals him actually to be Alexander The Great (Mr A.T. Great).

The final two-part sketch sees a man named Mr Notlob (Bolton backwards, as used in the 'Parrot Sketch', who sees a psychiatrist because he keeps hearing folk songs. He is referred to a surgeon ('who has a very similar office to this one'), who then operates only to find squatters in his abdomen. The surgical staff obtain a court order to evict them but end up sending the police in. After the final credits, there is one final 'intermission', followed by the foot coming down, and signifying the end of the series.

Comments.

Some things in the 'Historical Impersonations' sketch may need clarification for either younger or non-British viewers. Eddie Waring was known for commentating on Rugby League matches on the BBC (hence his character uttering 'Wigan, Hunslet and Hull Kingston Rovers'). Brian London was a boxer active in the '50s and '60s, and Freeman Hardy Willis was a chain of UK show shops common to most towns at the time. They finally closed in 1996.

Carol Cleveland plays several parts in this episode, including the Nurse in the 'Me, Doctor' routine, the hippie woman in Mr Notlob's abdomen and the psychiatrist's receptionist. Other parts, such as the women being led out in the raid on the restaurant, are uncredited. David Ballantyne plays the part of Ivan The Terrible.

The word 'albatross' is uttered thirteen times in this episode. This constitutes a record for the most times the word has been spoken on television in 30 minutes. Probably.

Author's Pick.

This is a hard one to pick a standout from, as it is an exceptionally strong episode. Clear highlights are the cannibal restaurant, the historical impersonations and the outrageous slapstick of the police using the power of magic. However, by a very short head, I will vote for the restaurant, if only for the incredible vision of a near-naked Terry Jones wheeled in with an apple (or tomato) in his mouth and also the glorious Fawlty-esque dialogue.

Series Two
All episodes produced and directed by Ian MacNaughton

It is common knowledge that certain factions at the BBC were less than happy about *Python*'s lampooning of the Corporation's programmes and of the organisation itself, and Chapman remarked sometime later that, even when they were successful, they always felt a little as if they were restricted to the shed, well away from the main house. However, there was a groundswell of a cult following already, and the press was largely enamoured of this ground-breaking outfit, so a second series was duly commissioned.

All was far from entirely rosy, however. The second series episodes were mainly broadcast at just after 10 pm on a Tuesday night, which in itself was a reasonable slot for this kind of fare. However, the broadcast schedule was wildly inconsistent. There were weeks when the show wasn't screened at all (including a notable clash with the *Horse Of The Year Show*), while Scotland had its own schedule separate from England and Wales, and in some areas it would be at the mercy of regional programming.

Episode One: Dinsdale
First aired 15 September 1970
Sketches include:
Face The Press
New Cooker Sketch
Tobacconist's
Ministry Of Silly Walks
The Piranha Brothers

Synopsis:
There are a couple of slight changes here for the new series, as the intro has Cleese sitting behind a desk in a cage announcing 'And now...', before the camera pans to the left to show our old friend in the next cage continuing '... it's...' and the opening credit sequence rolling. This is also changed, with the foot coming down twice, once midway, and the animation, particularly after that point, being very different to the previous series. The first sketch is 'Meet The Press', which features a debate between, on the government side, the Secretary Of State For Home Affairs (an outrageously drag-attired Chapman) and, against the government, 'a small patch of brown liquid'. It is entertaining, if insubstantial, but leads into the well-remembered 'New Cooker Sketch' featuring a cooker delivery running into problems with the paperwork as more and more gas-men appear in the house to suggest yet more forms and regulations. Eventually, the solution decided upon is to kill the customer with gas, which will apparently make 'Head Office be here by two'. We cut away from the house to see a line of identically attired gas-men lined up down the street, and into the tobacconist's shop where we find Idle desperately

asking one by one whether any of the advertisements in the window are for 'shady women' offering their services. After searching for double-entendres in such phrases as 'chest of drawers', 'pram for sale' and 'blood donor', he is eventually baffled by the meaning of 'blonde prostitute will indulge in any sexual activity for four quid a week'.

At this point, Cleese enters to buy a newspaper, and we are into perhaps the most famous of all *Python* routines, the 'Ministry Of Silly Walks'. Cleese's walk is still something astonishing to behold, and he makes the sketch what it is entirely by the genius of his performance. An explanation of an Anglo-French walk then follows, by the same moustache-sharing Frenchmen that we saw back in Episode Two of the first series, with the flying sheep. Note that as Cleese walks to the Ministry, he passes another long line of gas-men.

Following this, is one lengthy, final sketch with a BBC programme for some reason entitled 'Ethel The Frog' holding an investigation into British gangland violence. This centres on the notorious Piranha brothers, Doug and Dinsdale, with interviews provided by their nemesis, Superintendent Harry 'Snapper' Organs, and some of their erstwhile associates. The latter all lavish them with praise, and only under duress do they admit to the fact that the brothers regularly nailed their heads to the floor. Two of the people speaking in this segment were previously seen in the first series, as the Criminologist is introduced as 'The Amazing Kargol And Janet', while Luigi Vercotti, the unscrupulous manager of daredevil Ron Obvious also makes a return. We learn that one of the brothers, Dinsdale, had a paranoid fear whereby he imagined an enormous hedgehog called Spiny Norman who was out to get him.

As the (redesigned and more professional) credits roll, we see various shots of Spiny Norman appearing from behind buildings snarling 'Dinsdale!', before Cleese in the cage again makes a loud lion's roar, and we see the 'IT's' man now as a fully clothed skeleton.

Comments.

The corner shop where Cleese buys his newspaper at the beginning of 'Silly Walks' is in the same street as the 'New Cooker Sketch' house. It was a Newsagent's called Pickfords in Willesden, London, but is now a family home. The back yard in the Cooker Sketch is not the same row of houses; it is filmed in another terraced street around two miles north of the exterior front.

One of the cards in the newsagent's reads 'Wanted: 2 rooms with view of sewer. Need not be best view. Partial sufficient'. The man who Cleese meets at the Ministry asking for a grant to develop the silly walk he is working on is referred to as 'Mr Pewtey', which indicates he is a return of Palin's character from the 'Marriage Guidance Counsellor' sketch back in the second episode.

The bizarrely-named 'Ethel The Frog' current affairs programme in the 'Piranha Brothers' sketch was, unlikely as it sounds, responsible for the name of a heavy metal band in the late '70s and early '80s. Ethel The Frog, from Hull, formed in 1976 and released their only album in 1980. The programme mentioned as being on BBC2, 'the semi-final of Episode 3 of 'Kierkegaard's Journals', starring Richard Chamberlain, Peggy Mount and Billy Bremner' may warrant some further explanation, as Peggy Mount was a highly unglamorous sitcom actress of the time – and as far removed from Richard Chamberlain as you could get – while Billy Bremner was a short, red-haired footballer who captained Leeds United and Scotland. He was known for his short stature and explosive temper on the field.

The 'Ministry Of Silly Walks' has spawned many, many references, from such diverse things as episodes of *The Simpsons, Futurama* and *The Golden Girls* through to video games and a strip in the *Beano Book*. However, surely the two most unlikely must be a Belgian advertisement campaign for the Eurostar train service between Brussels and London and, most surreal of all, the small Norwegian town of Orje which introduced a pedestrian crossing on which it was mandatory to adopt a silly walk to cross!

The Piranha Brothers are loosely based on the London gangsters The Kray Twins, of course. Harry 'Snapper' Organs is himself, based on the policeman leading the Kray investigation, Leonard 'Nipper' Read.

Actress Daphne Davey appears very briefly in this episode, as Mrs Twolumps, the secretary to Mr Teabags (Cleese) at the Ministry, but this is uncredited. It is the only female performance in the episode and her sole *Python* appearance. Born in 1909, her only credited TV appearance came in an episode of *The Troubleshooters* in 1965. David Ballantyne, John Hughman and Stanley Mason appear as three of the gas-men in the cooker sketch. They all had repeated guest appearances on *Python*, but all fell off the acting world soon afterwards, by all accounts.

Author's Pick.
A very strong episode to begin the second series of *Python*, the accolade can nevertheless only really go to the 'Ministry For Silly Walks', if only for Cleese's bravura performance – though the historical footage of archive walks is also hilarious.

Episode Two: The Spanish Inquisition
First aired 22 September 1970
Sketches include:
The Spanish Inquisition
Jokes and Novelties Salesman
Tax on Thingy
Photos of Uncle Ted / The Spanish Inquisition (continued)
The Semaphore Version of Wuthering Heights
Court Charades
Race Against the Credits

Synopsis:
One of the greatest of all *Python* episodes, the titular 'Spanish Inquisition'

routines dominate, but elsewhere there is great material. Even the opening sequence is a classic, showing Jones as a man with handle-powered wings on his back desperately attempting man-powered flight, running across the horizon. Eventually we see him apparently flying across the ground at a low altitude until the picture rotates 90 degrees and it becomes clear that he was actually plummeting as he lands headfirst in the sand at the foot of a tall cliff. Other planted would-be aviators fill the scene, along with Cleese at a desk announcing 'And Now For Something Completely Different' and the 'It's' man popping up for his line.

From here, it is straight into the first 'Spanish Inquisition' sketch, as Chapman enters a room in Jarrow, 1912, to inform his wife that 'One on't cross beams gone owt askew on treadle!!'. When she pushes him as what on earth this means, he says that he didn't expect the Spanish Inquisition and Cardinals Ximinez, Biggles and Fang (Palin, Jones, Gilliam) burst in and deliver the immortal 'Nobody expects the Spanish Inquisition!' line. At first their chief weapon is announced to be 'surprise', but as more weapons are thought of, they go out and come in again, this time ending up with 'Among our weaponry are such diverse elements as...' before a list is read out. Ximinez demands the rack, at which point a hapless Biggles (with flying helmet) brandishes a wire dish-drying rack, which they gamely tie her to, before making a pitiful mime of turning the non-existent handle.

Chapman is, at this point, removed from the scene by Cleese who calls at the door asking whether he will open a door in another scene to help out. He agrees, and they travel by van to a house where he indeed opens the door to Idle as a travelling naughty novelty salesman. At the end of his patter he expects a punchline, to which Chapman asks Cleese if there is one. Apparently there is, and it is hilarious, but they forgot to tell him. As his next favour, he allows them to saw his head off, which then appears in a Gilliam animated sequence, leading via bizarrely edited vintage nude photos to a Civil Service committee room where several men discuss a 'tax on thingy', but argue about what 'thingy' entails.

After some vox pops about taxes', including the 'It's' man actually getting a line ('I would tax Raquel Welch. But I've a feeling she'd tax me'), we cut to a scene where a bored Carol Cleveland is being shown endless photos of 'Uncle Ted' by an older woman (played by Marjorie Wilde), and ripping them up as they are passed to her. The 'Spanish Inquisition' line is delivered again, and they burst in as before, this time tying up the old woman and asking her to confess to heresy, as they torture her by poking her with soft cushions and making her sit in a comfy chair. When she does the latter, Biggles himself breaks down and confesses.

This leads us to another *Python* classic, 'The Semaphore Version Of *Wuthering Heights*', which begins with the star-crossed lovers signalling 'Oh Catherine' and 'Oh Heathcliffe' to each other with subtitled semaphore flags. Catherine's husband appears at the door signalling her and repeating it with enormous flags when she appears to be ignoring him. Finally, Catherine (Cleveland) confronts her husband with a brilliantly delivered long and impassioned speech while frantically marching up and down in fury. This leads into excerpts from '*Julius Caesar* On An Aldis Lamp', '*Gunfight At The OK Corral* In Morse Code' and finally 'The Smoke Signal Version of *Gentlemen Prefer Blondes*'.

A courtroom scene where all of the announcements are made in the form of Charades leads into the Inquisition line being delivered again, as all turn to look at the door and we see the three Cardinals rushing out of a house, boarding a bus while checking urgently where the rolling credits are up to, and finally bursting into the courtroom just as the credits end with 'Nobody expects... Oh, bugger!'

Comments.

Carol Cleveland plays no less than four separate characters in this episode, namely the young women in both 'Spanish Inquisition' episodes, Catherine in Wuthering Heights and Second Counsel in the courtroom. The only other guest parts are Marjorie Wilde as the old lady and an uncredited woman as a sexy courtroom exhibit. Wilde was born in 1901 and had a great many minor TV roles from 1946 through to her final role in *The Liver Birds* in 1976.

The music playing as the Inquisition race desperately against the closing credits is 'Devil's Galop' by Charles Williams, best known as the theme music to the post-war radio series *Dick Barton – Special Agent*.

The Semaphore Version Of *Wuthering Heights* is 'Presented by Twentieth Century Vole', a reference to the fictional film company from Episode Six of the first series. The semaphore signalling done by the characters is partly accurate, with the male characters accurately signalling some of the shorter lines but 'busking' the longer ones, but Cleveland's Catherine just signals random letters. In order for her final indignant 'rant' to be effective, this would be unavoidable anyway.

The house where Idle is the novelty salesman is located in Ealing, just across the road from Walpole Park, where parts of 'Bicycle Repair Man', 'Hell's Grannies' and 'The Dull Life Of A City Stockbroker' were filmed.

Author's Pick.

The Semaphore *Wuthering Heights* is a rightly-lauded masterpiece, from the huge flags used by Cathy's husband to call louder, through the sleeping man's signalling of 'Zzzz' to Carol Cleveland's hilarious furiously-pacing signalling that borders on genius, but it has to just lose out to the inspired lunacy of the Spanish Inquisition. The reach and influence of that sketch are so profound that 'Nobody expects the Spanish Inquisition' has almost become a quasi-historical phrase, and the soft pillows and comfy chair, together with the list of 'chief weapons' are happily quoted to this day by almost as many people as the Parrot Sketch. Definitive *Python*, from an episode with an embarrassment of riches.

Episode Three: Déjà Vu
First aired 29 September 1970
Sketches include:
Flying Lessons
Hijacked Plane
The Poet Ewan McTeagle
Psychiatrist Milkman
Déjà Vu

Synopsis:
We open with a window in a high rise building, which is opened by a woman (Cleveland) who complains how hot it is before beginning to remove her clothes. As she reaches her stockings, a window-cleaning cradle ascends into view carrying Cleese, whose 'And now for something completely different' line is met by a woodland scene complete with animals, in which a deer immediately explodes. Cut back to a confused Cleese and a still disrobing (but largely out of shot) Cleveland for 'And now for something more completely different' and quick cut to 'It's' man close up.

The first sketch proper sees an owl follow the unfortunate deer to explosive extinction before we see a bishop in full robes rehearsing the line 'Oh Mr Belpit, your legs are so swollen' in a field, repeatedly in different voices. Mr Chigger (Jones) approaches him asking about flying lessons. He explains it is nothing to do with him as 'This is show five, I'm not in until show eight'. Chigger then finds a secretary (Cleveland) in the middle of the field, and she leads him through the countryside past such office trappings as a hallway meeting in a stream and a tea trolley in another field, before going underground and emerging from a tent in a shopping street. They enter a building where he is handed over to another identical secretary and shown into an office where Mr Anemone (Chapman) is dangling from the ceiling from wires on the phone. He attempts to instruct Mr Chiggers by making him flap his arms and jump off the desk, and ridicules his desire for an aeroplane while insisting his clearly visible wire does not exist.

We cut forward to a cockpit scene captioned as two years hence, with Chiggers flying the plane, but this is interrupted by Idle as a pedantic airline official with 'wing-commander' moustache who clarifies that it takes six years to become an airline pilot. The caption changes to read 'Four years later than the previous caption' which Idle approves off before launching into a litany of other continuity errors which have irritated him. This forms a running gag of complaints in the episode (as well as exploding animals). After another Chapman character mistakes the cockpit for the toilet and walks out of the exterior door, landing unhurt in some hay outside a public toilet, Palin enters as a useless hijacker who demands, in bumbling fashion, that they reroute the plane to Luton (it is, of course, headed to Cuba). They compromise and drop him out of the plane over a haystack near Basingstoke. He boards a bus reading

'Straight to Luton', which is immediately hijacked at gunpoint by another man and diverted to Cuba.

After a sketch featuring a celebration of the Scottish poet Ewan McTeagle and his masterpieces such as 'Lend me a quid until the end of the week', culminating in a Scotsman delivering another barrage of continuity complaints (before Palin emerges from under his kilt with a stethoscope, announcing that he is a doctor, before stating that he is actually a gynaecologist, but this is his lunch hour), and a rather impressive Gilliam animation of hands as trees and another hand as a horse ridden by a cowboy, we cut to a woman (Mrs Ratbag) who is visited by Idle dressed as a milkman who claims to be a psychiatrist.

He takes her to his 'psychiatry float', past a cat which immediately blows up, and they drive off before being stopped by Palin's doctor character who needs an emergency psychiatrist, as his usual – Jersey Cream Psychiatrists – have not turned up. He is taken by a milkmaid complete with pails and a yoke who leads him across the same countryside traversed earlier by Mr Chigger, replete again with office staff, in order to see a psychiatrist (Dr Cream), who is talking to a cow named Audrey which is lying upside down on his couch.

Another bewildering array of people complaining about the programme and more exploding woodland animals leads into the final sketch, with a TV programme called 'It's The Mind', sees Plain discussing Déjà Vu, before being subjected to, and terrified by, an escalating series of such repeating episodes.

Comments.
During the 'Psychiatrist Milkman' sketch, Jones' character changes from Mrs Ratbag at the start of the sketch to being referred to as Mrs Pim later in it. There is no apparent explanation for this, so it may actually be a continuity error, or it may be a deliberately inserted one so that it is juxtaposed against the heap of continuity and research complaints during the episode. The latter does seem more likely. Notably, the Milk Float scenes were filmed in Torquay in May, at the end of a week's shooting during which the party started off staying at the Gleneagles Hotel, run by a Mr Sinclair – a man so rude that while the rest of the cast moved out after one day, Cleese stayed there to get ideas. Thus was born *Fawlty Towers*.

There is another bumper array of roles for Cleveland this week, as she plays the girl in the window, secretary, aeroplane stewardess and milkmaid, with the only other guest turn coming from Jeanette Wild who has the small part of the second secretary.

The rehearsing bishop states that this is show five, and he isn't in until show eight, but of course this is only show number three and, naturally, his big appearance never happens. We never do discover the mystery of Mr Belpit's legs.

Apparently, the 'Election Night Special' was originally planned for this episode, but the Déjà Vu material got a little out of hand, and so it was put back for three episodes.

Near the end of the psychiatrist sketch, Mrs Pim is invited to 'walk this way', before being stopped with wagging fingers when beginning the inevitable punchline of 'if I could walk that way' etc.' This begins a running gag throughout the next two episodes

Author's Pick.
A good quality show, if an inevitable step down from the previous episode, the pick here is the 'Déjà Vu' sketch, if only for Palin's masterful comic performance as he becomes ever more unnerved and startled by repeating events. In fact, with his airline hijacker also a brilliant portrayal, this is very much Palin's show in terms of performance.

Episode Four: The Buzz Aldrin Show
First aired 20 October 1970
Sketches include:
Architects Sketch
Motor Insurance Sketch
The Bishop
Living Room on Pavement
Poets
Chemist Sketch

Synopsis:
There is an unusual animated opening here, as a caterpillar/man hybrid goes to bed and wakes up as a resplendent butterfly/man. At this point, in a perfect example of the primitive nature of early 'green screen' effects work, Cleese hovers up at a rotor-powered desk and delivers the 'And Now...' announcement. A rather laborious Gumby announcement featuring all five main cast in unison introduces the 'Architects Sketch', with Chapman as Mr Tid, introducing two prospective architects for a new block of flats to his colleagues. Cleese enters first, beginning well but soon making it clear, by the references to rotating knives, blood and soundproofing, that he has actually designed an abattoir by mistake. When the clients insist that they really want flats rather than slaughtering their tenants, he launches into a tirade against them which turns into him begging them to accept him as a Freemason. He is shown out, and Idle enters, demonstrating his large 28-storey tower block, the model of which immediately lists precariously and then bursts into flames. In a rather chilling foreshadowing of the Grenfell Tower fire in London in 2017, the clients accept it as it is when told that safety features would be expensive, as the word 'Satire' flashes up on screen. They finally exchange 'Masonic' handshakes with Idle. It's very funny, but also in the contemporary climate it is somewhat uncomfortable and sobering.
    The sketch develops into an outdoor scene showing how to recognise a Mason, with businessmen hopping to work without trousers and other men writhing on the floor outside an office building, delivering elaborate

handshakes with rolled-up trouser legs. An announcement apologising for this follows the running joke of the episode, which is 'Apologies', but one senses it also had a purpose in terms of covering the collective backs of the BBC. Next we are into the 'Motor Insurance Sketch', again introduced by the rather tiresome Gumby collective, where Mr Devious explains to his customer (Chapman) about his various policy offers, including a nude lady and a selection of dirty books. Next in is Idle as Reverend Morrison who is concerned about a letter threatening to fill his mouth with cement. He is informed that, despite his car being hit by a lorry while in his garage, he cannot claim. This is because he has purchased the 'Neverpay policy', which is cheap as long as you don't try to claim – absurd, but not that far away from 'no claims bonuses' if you think about it.

The appearance of Jones as a fearsome-looking bishop leads into the hilarious 'Bishop' sketch, an outdoor extravaganza in which Jones, in full regalia, supported by a posse of black-clad priests, rushes from one ecclesiastical emergency to the next, always arriving just too late. The credits, designed by Gilliam, are a work of art in themselves, perfectly parodying 1960s TV shows such as *Man In A Suitcase*. From this, we cut to a middle-aged couple, the Potters (Palin and Chapman) who are living, surrounded by furniture, on the pavement, We are told that the builders have not yet arrived. When Mrs Potter opens the door to go to the 'bathroom', she discovers Alfred Lord Tennyson in the bathtub, and we are into the 'Poets' sketch, wherein Palin comes to read the poet of randy housewife Jones, in the manner of reading the meter. He is a 'Wordsworth' and is installed under the stairs. After she seduces him, we are into the three-part 'Chemist Sketch', during which the BBC apologise for some of the language used. The shop changes to a 'Less Naughty Chemist' and finally a 'Not At All Naughty Chemist', with Idle as a customer trying to buy some aftershave containing either halibut or sea bass. After Chapman enters as a - clearly insane - policeman, there is an apology for a reference to astronaut Buzz Aldrin, and the credits roll detailing Aldrin heavily involved in the writing and crew for the 'Buzz Aldrin Show'.

Comments.

In a big change from the previous show, Carol Cleveland has no appearance this week, with the only female role, in the Chemist sketch, played by the unknown Sandra Richards, in her only credited TV appearance. Stanley Mason plays the absurd shoplifter's accomplice in the same sketch.

The words banned by the BBC during the Chemist sketch are as follows: B*m, P*tty, P*x, Kn*ckers, Kn*ckers, W**-W** and Semprini. The latter was, bizarrely, an English pianist and composer known for his regular BBC radio work.

References to other episodes abound here, particularly during the Chemist sketch, with Palin announcing that he didn't expect the Spanish Inquisition (then, because he said the line himself, being told to shit up), suggesting to the aftershave customer that he has some 'Parrot', and also the 'If I could walk that way...' joke again being stopped before the punchline. Elsewhere, when people are asked for their choices of aftershave, one of those is Cardinal Ximinez, who repeats the joke of finding more varieties to say every time he lists them, and also Ron Shabby, from Series One.

The music playing during the 'Bishop' sketch, as they chase around frantically, is the *Peter Gunn* theme by Henry Mancini – later to be recorded by Progressive Rock band Emerson Lake And Palmer, bizarrely enough.

Note that there was a three-week gap between this and the previous episode. This was because the BBC, in their infinite wisdom, elected to scrap the show for two weeks in order to accommodate coverage of the *Horse Of The Year Show*. This was not received in the most positive light by the team, who presented their grudges in no uncertain terms – to no avail, of course.

Author's Pick.
A very, very strong show, with only the Gumby links misfiring somewhat, and even Gilliam's animations are some of his best work, with a scenario of two men bouncing up and down on an enormous woman being especially memorable. As a result, choosing a favourite sketch is enormously difficult, and it is almost a three-way tie between the Architects, the Bishop and the Chemist's. By a very, very small margin I will award it to 'The Bishop', one of the most 'laugh-out-loud' sequences ever filmed by the Pythons.

Episode Five: Live From The Grill-o-Mat
First aired 27 October 1970
Sketches include:
Blackmail
Society for Putting Things on Top of Other Things
Accidents Sketch
Seven Brides for Seven Brothers
The Butcher Who is Alternately Rude and Polite
Ken Clean-Air System

Synopsis:
Opening this episode is Cleese in the Grill-o-Mat Snack Bar, Paignton (a typically shabby greasy-spoon cafe), sitting at one of the plastic tables next to two customers and doing the link announcements with very forced bonhomie and good humour. This forms one of the two running gags for the episode, and he introduces both the title sequence and the first item proper, which is the 'Blackmail Sketch'. Introduced by Palin's typically smooth TV announcer, it consists of viewers having to send in money in order to prevent their identities being revealed and, in the best-remembered sequence, a film which has to be stopped by telephone as the money required increases like a taxi meter.

The link to the next item is that the man who phones in to stop the film (Jones) is actually in the next sketch when he calls. This is the absurd 'Society For Putting Things On Top Of Other Things' and features a group of extremely pompous men in evening dress at a dinner at which Chapman speaks grandly and portentously about the success and lack thereof over the last year vis-a-vis putting things on top of other things. Called to task for his area's failure, Cleese gives the excuse that his members feel it is all rather silly, at which point all agree, and the meeting dissolves. Things get rather self-referential now as the men, led by Chapman, realise they are being filmed from outside and elect to tunnel out under a vaulting horse, accompanied by two German prison guards who have appeared.

For the viewer, who may feel that this is becoming uncomfortably like a vivid dream following a surfeit of cheese, there is sadly no escape from this impression, as the men find another way out, emerge in an animation scene and fall through a hole. They then spend the next several sketch links travelling through the digestive system, being fired at on a cloud and other uncomfortable scrapes before eventually emerging later in the show. This, along with Cleese's announcer, who also pops up regularly, is the other running gag. In between this utter mayhem, the next sketch sees Idle as a man shown into a rather grand room in a mansion house to await a meeting. Every time he is left alone in the room by the long-suffering if sardonic butler (Chapman) a disaster happens. A mirror falls off the wall, a large dresser unit topples over, the maid sent to tidy up (Cleveland) impales herself on a dagger she has given him to hold, a further member of staff falls out of the window, and finally a policeman comes to arrest him has a heart attack. He then runs from the scene, only for the house to explode behind him.

The men from the animation emerge and run past him, looking for a school, which we see is presenting a performance of *Seven Brides For Seven Brothers*, which collapses in on itself when most of the pupils fail to turn up, and we are left with two brides and four brothers. Following more animated insanity involving a piggy-bank hunt with hammers, we cut to a butcher's shop during which the entire routine is based around the butcher (Idle) and his alternately rude and polite responses to Palin, the customer. Following this is the final routine, telling the story of champion (though 'almost completely stupid') boxer Ken Clean-Air System and his training regime as he prepares to fight Cliff Richard-loving schoolgirl Connie Booth for a hilariously mismatched contest. After this, we are back to the apologetic and uncomfortable Cleese who is by now on the bus going home.

Comments.
Carol Cleveland and Connie Booth handle almost all of the female parts between them this week (the latter playing the boxer's opponent and one of the Seven Brides), with the only credited exception being the second schoolgirl played by Lyn Ashley, a regular small-parter in TV shows in the '60s and '70s, and who was married to Eric Idle at the time. She is credited as 'Mrs Idle', as indeed she will be in several more episodes in which she appears going forward.

Three links from previous episodes crop up, here. Firstly, during the 'Society' sketch, the 'If I could walk that way' routine is done for the third and final time, and secondly the rehearsing Bishop from Episode Three is encountered by the animation escapees still declaiming about poor Mr Belpit's swollen legs. Note that this time it IS show number five, but despite his belief that he will be in 'next week', he won't be. The third and final example of this is the short link with Cleese and Idle as flatmates Mr Praline and Brooky who are given a chat show which is then immediately cancelled. They go on to play the piano at the school play. Cleese's Mr Praline is dressed in exactly the same outfit as he wears in the 'Parrot Sketch'.

The two animated characters, Neddy and Teddy, who go on the piggy-bank hunt, are in fact both represented by photographs of US Civil War Union military figure Benjamin Franklin Butler. So, neither Neddy nor Teddy.

The nude organist during the Blackmail programme, Mr Onan, is on this occasion portrayed by Terry Gilliam.

For those interested in such things, the open-top bus on which Cleese delivers his closing announcement is apparently a Devon General 'Sea Dog' class open-top Leyland Atlantean/Metro-Cammell, en route between Paignton and Babbacombe. So there.

Author's Pick.
A less than classic episode, and much of this one fails to hit the spot. The 'Blackmail' sketch is still well-regarded, but has not stood the test of time as well as other celebrated *Python* items. The Idle 'Accidents' routine and the abusive butcher have their moments, but I will give the pick of this episode to the 'Ken Clean-Air System' documentary, if only for the classic running into a parked car, being confused, and turning round to run the other way. Additionally, the fight scene at the end is so ridiculous as to be laugh-out-loud funny. In a way, the well-executed Cleese running gag with the uncomfortable links actually serves to hinder the flow, even though it is not only deliberate but also extremely well done, which is somewhat ironic.

Episode Six: It's A Living
First aired 3 November 1970
Sketches include:
It's a Living
The Time on BBC 1
School Prize-Giving
Mr Dibley
The Foreign Secretary
Free Dung
Timmy Williams
Raymond Luxury Yacht
Marriage Registry office
Election Night Special

Synopsis:
Another rather hit-and-miss episode here, though notable for the team beginning to play a little more 'fast and loose' with the show format. The usual introduction is wholly dispensed with, as a faux-TV programme called 'It's A Living' opens things up by discussion of the BBC's fee system. It then cuts to the BBC1 'globe' which used to be the background to between-show links, with Palin rambling about time in a surreal manner. This cuts, via some odd animation involving climbing into Enoch Powell's head, into the theme music which is in darkness until around halfway through, when someone manages to turn on the lights. Cleese then appears, apologising for not delivering his 'Completely Different' line because he is 'not in the show' this week. It then goes over to a school prize-giving ceremony which effectively consists of various criminals fighting each other for the prizes and ends in a pitched gun battle.

This bears a resemblance to the then-topical film *If* – deliberately so, as it leads into Jones as Mr LF Dibley, a film director who manages to produce hopeless versions of classic films just too late. The school scene is from his own *If*, but we learn he was also just too late with his versions of *2001*, *Midnight Cowboy* and *Rear Window*, which simply features a man looking out of a rear window. He accepts that his *Finian's Rainbow*, starring 'The man from the off-license' was a disaster. We are shown a clip. It is.

The interviewer now cuts to a report from the Foreign Secretary about canoeing. An outside shot sees the FS himself in a canoe on a riverbank. Two men, in what appears to be Arab dress rush on, pick up canoe, Secretary and all, and hurl them in the water, before running off cackling at high speed. Following a demonstration of a human pyramid by three key figures in the field of Industrial Relations, it is back to throwing things in the water, as the odd men give the same treatment to large wicker baskets containing the President of the Board Of Trade and the Vice Chairman of ICI. Cyclist Reg Harris, complete with bicycle, is the next to be hurled in before two baskets containing singers Anne Ziegler and Webster Booth follow suit. The speeded-up film and bizarre sound, make these scenes very funny. The sketch ends with an 85-year-old woman, Dame Irene Stoat, reciting her poetry on the near bank, which leaves the 'hit squad' on the far bank very frustrated. Fortunately, a screaming Samurai warrior is on hand to push her in.

Following a short animation featuring a fully motorised pig, we cut to a rather civilised dinner party at which Cleese arrives with a large delivery of dung. It turns out this was a free gift with the Book Of The Month club, along with the dead American Indian (who is merely stunned) which came with their cooker. Idle is up next as Timmy Williams, an utterly self-absorbed and smarmy media figure who meets Jones at a restaurant, but fails to take in the latter's sad tale about his dead wife as he is greeting people and taking phone calls the whole time. Jones finally shoots himself.

Two short items follow this – firstly, a single-joke effort with Chapman as a man with an enormous false nose being interviewed until he announces that his name, though spelt Raymond Luxury-Yacht, is actually pronounced Throatwobbler Mangrove. This leads into a rather feeble bit with a marriage registrar and confusion over the request to him of 'Will you marry me?' The reply of 'I'm sorry sir, I am married already' is not particularly funny to start with and only gets worse.

Still, we are hurtling toward the endgame now, with a hastily-edited Gilliam animation (see below) leading into the famed 'Election Night Special', which retains many moments of genius but overall has been performed in longer and more satisfying arrangements in many future live airings. Time has not been kind to this original recording.

Comments.
The Gilliam animation before the Election sketch originally featured a fairy tale about a prince who ignored a spot on his face, followed by the rather controversial line 'three years later he died of cancer'. Clearly finding this in rather bad taste, the BBC had the word 'cancer' replaced for all future repeats and video releases, though the wholly out of place dubbing of the word 'gangrene' makes it appear as if this dreadfully executed dub was the Pythons making a point.

The celebrated 'silly party' candidate name Tarquin Fin-tim-lin-bin-whin-bim-lim-bus-stop-F'tang-F'tang-Olé-Biscuitbarrel achieved a belated second life in 1981 when a student named John Dougrez-Lewis changed his name to it by deed poll before contesting the Crosby by-election. He received 223 votes and finished fifth out of nine. The full name was printed on the ballot paper but the Returning Officer, somewhat disappointingly, referred to him only as 'Tarquin Biscuitbarrel'. In the same sketch, Cleese asks the question 'What do you make of the nylon dog cardigan and plastic mule rest?' These items were originally named in a Goon Show sketch from 1956, and this is acknowledged in the comment 'Thank you, Spike'. Finally, in the result Engelbert Humperdinck gains Barrow In Furness from Ann Haydon-Jones and her husband Pip, Haydon-Jones refers to the English tennis player Ann Jones and her husband Philip 'Pip' Jones, also a tennis player.

Rita Davies makes another appearance here, as the hostess at the dinner party. This is her first since the 'Hell's Grannies' sketch in the first series. She was married to *Python* producer Ian McNaughton.

In the 'human pyramid', Ray Millichope is named as the leader of the Allied Technicians' Union. This was an 'in-joke' tribute, as he was the Series Editor of *Python* and later many other shows including *The Two Ronnies*.

Author's Pick.
One would probably expect 'Election Night Special' to be the clear winner here from this patchy episode, but such is not the case. I am going to plump for the brilliantly directed and edited 'Foreign Secretary' sketch, which manages

to make the simple repetitive gag of throwing people into the water somehow hilarious. 'Election Night' is certainly classic, but I feel the *Live At Drury Lane* version, in particular, to be far more impressive, in terms of writing and performance.

Episode Seven: The Attila The Hun Show
First aired 10 November 1970
Sketches include:
The Attila The Hun Show
Secretary of State Striptease
Ratcatcher
Killer Sheep
The News for Parrots
The Idiot in Rural Society
Test Match Against Iceland
Spot The Braincell

Synopsis:
This episode begins in a highly unconventional manner (that is to say, what would soon become perfectly conventional for *Python*) by appearing to be another programme entirely. This programme is 'The Attila The Hun Show', hilariously spoofing safe, American family shows of the time with the 'Hun' family gathering in the living room to discuss conquest and massacre. Cleese is especially hilarious as Attila himself, being pushed on the swing by his laughing family.

Following this, we, at last, get the credits, followed by a hospital scene where, via a quick 'Attila The Nun' gag, we have Carol Cleveland as a sexy patient having her chest examined to the accompaniment of striptease music while a cluster of voyeurs with hands thrust in dirty raincoats look on. This leads on to the unedifying spectacle of Terry Jones performing a full-on burlesque striptease act as the Secretary Of State for Commonwealth Affairs while delivering a speech.

Moving swiftly along, we meet Eric Idle as a ratcatcher come to address a family's rodent problem. He initially announces as a joke that he has come to tell them that the forthcoming Third Test Match against the West Indies will be played in their flat, before revealing who he actually is. While looking for the signs of infestation, there is much digression about the word 'wainscoting', and the residents of a Dorset village of that name, excited to be mentioned. Predictably, a bunch of cricketers led by Cleese enter asking if this where the match is to be played. It soon comes to light that this is, in fact, a sheep infestation, borne out by an enormous hole. He enters the hole only to flee out after gunfire erupts. These sheep are, unusually, armed, and this leads to a laboratory where the Killer Sheep are being investigated, via another gag whereby opening the door to another lab reveals it to be full of cricketers, led by a blacked-up Cleese asking if the Third Test is going to be played there. We then go completely down the rabbit-hole into an inspired animation scene of the sheep mounting a series of daring heists, before an announcement about other freakishly intelligent species leads us into 'The News For Parrots', followed by the same for gibbons and wombats.

After an animated scene with a vicious bun (which is, of course, Attila The Bun), we have a classic Cleese portrayal of a traditional 'Village Idiot' who is extremely erudite and well-spoken in between bouts of inspired idiocy for the tourists. This takes us to the commentary box for, yes, the cricket – although this is the first test against Iceland, who have already scored 722 while England have now been batting for five hours without scoring. The commentary team - Cleese, Chapman and Idle - are surrounded by bottles as they enthusiastically praise nothing at all happening while Idle reels off endless tedious statistics. Finally, a Chesterfield sofa, complete with pads, comes in to bat, leading to the whole field being replaced by furniture and then a cut to a race at Epsom between, of course, furniture.

This inspired episode is finally wrapped up by 'Spot The Braincell', a TV game show based clearly on the *Take Your Pick* show which had recently come to an end after a number of years on British television. Cleese parodies that show's host Michael Miles brilliantly, while Jones plays the irredeemably stupid Mrs Scum who manages to win through to receive the star prize of 'a blow on the head'. Along the way Mrs Scum delivers a breathtakingly racist line which would never get written today, yet is extremely funny in the context – one would guess that it escaped the censor's pen until now because the character is intended to be stupid. She manages to blindly guess the name of an obscure philosopher, yet has enormous trouble with the main food of penguins. Even after a Cleese mime of a fish, she is unable to get nearer than moussaka, lobster thermidore or Brian Close.

Comments.
The 'Attila The Hun' sketch is a clear spoof of the then-popular *Debbie Reynolds Show*, with the title scenes being a shot-for-shot parody. Even the theme music is a clear homage.

During the first run of repeats of this series, the 'Spot The Braincell' sketch (as it is generally known) was cut from the episode owing to the death of Michael Miles, the presenter of the original *Take Your Pick* programme. It was reinstated again after that. Note that a reference to 'Spam' was sneaked into that sketch before the actual 'Spam Song' made its *Python* debut. The sketch itself is not brand new, having already been done in radically different versions by Cleese and Tim Brooke-Taylor on *How To Irritate People*, and also on *At Last The 1948 Show*, with Marty Feldman.

The list of 'Brians' which are suggested as the chief food of penguins are: Brian Close (English cricketer), Brian Johnson (official sources suggest that this is a special effects man, best known at that time for his work on *Thunderbirds,* but given the huge number of cricket references in this episode, it's far more likely it's a mispronunciation of cricket commentator Brian Johnstone), Brian

Inglis (journalist and presenter of *All Our Yesterdays*) and Bryan Forbes (actor, director and then-head of EMI Films). Note that Forbes was married to Nanette Newman, who is herself suggested as an answer to the penguin question.

During the Furniture Race, one 'contestant' which may need explanation is 'Joanna Southcott's Box'. Joanna Southcott was a self-styled religious prophetess and writer who left a sealed box of prophecies after her death in 1814, to be opened at a time of national crisis in the company of all the Bishops of the Church Of England. It has never been opened and is rumoured to be held at a secret location. Southcott had over 100,000 followers at the time of her death and is mentioned in Charles Dickens' *A Tale Of Two Cities*. The box, however, finished in last place at Epsom, behind Wash Basin, WC Pedestal, Sofa, Hat Stand and Standard Lamp, so a poor showing there.

The cricketers behind Cleese looking for the test match are uncredited walk-ons for David Aldridge (*Dr Who*), Steve Smart, David Gilchrist (*Dad's Army*), Jim Haswell (*Dr Who*) and George Janson.

Author's Pick.
A sublime episode with so much inspired lunacy it is hard to pick a favourite, but despite the brilliance of the 'Attila The Hun Show' parody, the 'Killer Sheep' story, spread over animation and live-action, must take the honours. The sight of the sheep leaving the bank with firstly bags of money and then later a safe on their backs, is never to be forgotten.

Episode Eight: Archaeology Today
First aired 17 November 1970
Sketches Include:
Trailer
Archaeology Today
Silly Vicar
Wife Swap
Silly doctor sketch (immediately abandoned)
Mr and Mrs Git
Roy and Hank Spim – Mosquito hunters
Judges
Mrs Thing and Mrs Entity
Beethoven

Synopsis:
The episode begins with the BBC2 'Globe' and a bogus trailer read by Idle, for upcoming programmes, almost all of which are concerning sport, most being cricket. An exception is Lulu taking on The Old Man Of Hoy, on an edition of *Panorama* introduced by Tony Jacklin. If you have ever yearned to witness a comedy series starring Jim Laker called 'Thirteen Weeks Of Off-Spin Bowling', this will pique your interest. This leads into the credits (via a tiny

snippet of 'Saturday Sports' by Wilfred Burns – often mistakenly claimed to be the *Grandstand* theme), which ends with the foot crumbling and being absorbed into the ground, which sees two generations of buildings rise and fall before a single giant toe is excavated and believed to be the nose of a sort of elephant creature.

We are on firmer ground next (if you will pardon the pun) with the show 'Archaeology Today', in which presenter Palin is only obsessed with the height of his guests – the mere five foot ten Jones and the six-foot-five behemoth Cleese, upon whom he dotes. We then see a clip of a dig from 1920 with Cleese breaking into joyful song each time he digs something up. This is shattered when Palin appears, hoisting Jones upon his shoulders to beat the height of Cleese. His assistant climbs on his shoulders, they both also get a servant atop them, and they fight to the death.

A short sketch with Chapman as a mad vicar who is appealing for rights for the insane is followed up by Idle as a woman who has forgotten who she is, appealing for 'The National Truss'. She goes through several possible identities including singers Leapy Lee and PP Arnold, cricketer Sir Len Hutton and an early mention of Margaret Thatcher before she is felled by a boxer with a single punch. Next up is a man who arrived at a Wedding Registrar with a woman wanting to exchange the one he married on Saturday for this one. After a short while, a rude expletive is interrupted by Cleese rushing on as a referee and booking the man.

A Doctor sketch is next, which is very short and very silly revolving around misunderstood names, and is soon announced as 'abandoned'. We then move to a party where Jones is introduced to an uncomfortable Palin as 'A Snivelling Little Rat-Faced Git'. It turns out that 'Git' is his surname, with the rest being his forenames, and it is, of course, the 'Git' part which embarrasses him. His wife 'Dreary Fat Boring Old' (Cleese) is then introduced. Things become disgusting when the Gits begin talking with pride about their house which is 'smeared with warm pus', and the disembowelling party they are hosting with their friends the Nauseas, Mucuses and 'the Rectums from Swanage'. At that point the sketch is restarted in a 'clean version', a nun appears to state that she prefers the dirty version and she is immediately felled by the boxer.

A film of two Australian outback hunters going after a mosquito with missile launchers and heavy weaponry leads us, via a pair of camp judges, to the hilarious Beethoven sketch, which sees Cleese in a brilliant turn as the master attempting to get his Fifth Symphony perfected while his wife constantly interrupts him with questions about the kitchen and then entering with the vacuum cleaner. After we see other great figures struggling in similar domestic ways (Shakespeare doing the dishes, Michelangelo nursing several infants and Mozart cleaning the floor), Mozart's son Colin is introduced as a rat-catcher with his first client being the Beethovens. Ludwig is more fraught than ever as rats have infested his piano and are crawling all over his head as he continues to hammer away at the keys while complaining bitterly. The camp judges return to gossip over the end credits.

Comments.
Cleveland plays almost all of the female roles here, with the only exception being the replacement bride who is played by an uncredited Barbara Lindsey (she appeared in several films and TV shows up to 1974, with several episodes of *Up Pompeii* with Frankie Howerd to her name).

One of Gilliam's animated scenes in this episode concerns a gangster parody featuring a giant chicken followed around by eggs. He is named 'Eggs Diamond' after the notorious US mobster Legs Diamond. Spiny Norman the hedgehog also gets a repeat appearance, looming from behind a building calling 'Dinsdale!'

The notice board outside the Beethovens' residence, showing all of the occupants reads as follows: MR AND MRS EMMANUEL KANT, FRAU MITZI HANDGEPACKAUFBEWAHRUNG, MR DICKIE WAGNER, K. TYNAN (NO RELATION), MR AND MRS J. W. VON GOETHE AND DOG, HERR E. W. SWANTON, MR AND MRS P. ANKA, MR AND MRS LUDWIG VAN BEETHOVEN (1770-1827) ACCEPT NO SUBSTITUTE. The second of these translates as Frau Mitzi Left-Luggage Office, for no apparent reason.

The old, crackly sounding song mimed by Cleese during the Archaeology dig (beginning 'Today! I hear the robin sing!') is often assumed to be a genuine period recording from that time. In fact, it is an original song written by Musical Director Bill McGuffie, and sung by Jones and Cleveland.

Author's Pick.
This is a close one, with the 'Archaeology' sketch particularly impressive, but the honours must go to Cleese's hilarious performance as Beethoven. That whole sketch is classic *Python*.

Episode Nine: How To Recognise Different Parts Of The Body
First aired 24 November 1970
Sketches Include:
How to Recognise Different Parts of the Body
Bruces sketch
The Man who Contradicts People
Cosmetic Surgery
Camp Square-Bashing
Killer Cars (Animation)
Cut-Price Airline
Batley Townswomen's Guild Presents the First Heart Transplant
The Death of Mary Queen of Scots
There's Been a Murder

Synopsis:
The show opens this time with a bevvy of bikini-clad women. The camera lazily pans across them until it arrives on the less lovely bikini-clad form of Cleese on

his desk for his familiar announcement, cutting to the 'It's' man in... yes, you guessed it! The title sequence announces the show title, and accordingly, we are treated to a helpful arrow pointing us to several parts of the body, including red polka-dotted shorts identified as 'the naughty bits'. The first sketch proper is the well known 'Bruces' sequence with four Australian men (actually philosophy lecturers) all called Bruce and living up to every Antipodean stereotype known to man. Jones, an Englishman called Michael, arrives to join the team, clad in full business suit, and they announce they will call him Bruce to avoid confusion.

Via some more 'naughty bits' (those same shorts on a woman, a horse and Reginald Maudling) we arrive at a short sketch whereby a man who always contradicts people is interviewed by putting to him the opposite to the facts. This confusing scenario is soon ended with a gong, and we have the return of Chapman's Raymond Luxury-Yacht, he of the enormous nose and the name actually pronounced Throatwobbler Mangrove. He comes to see a specialist plastic surgeon (Cleese) who has so many qualifications that his nameplate stretches around three sides of the room and Chapman has to open a gate in it to enter. He spots that the nose is a huge polystyrene fake, but Throatwobbler still demands the operation. Cleese agrees, but only if they can go camping together. Cut to them bounding through the undergrowth in slow-motion bliss, hand in hand.

A short film – amusing, if hideously dated – of some outrageously camp square-bashing soldiers leads into the classic animation piece of the 'Killer Cars', with the cars in question hiding behind trees and buildings to leap out onto unsuspecting pedestrians. They are seen off by the greater problem of a giant cat stalking the city on its hind legs. The next sketch proper has Idle and Cleveland as passengers on a very suspect cut-price airline. They are sold very cheap tickets before being shown through to another room where they are offered duty-free broccoli and Eccles cakes to an allowance of 200 per person, distracting them while the tail of the plane is carried through and a hysterically ranting Kamikaze pilot is ushered past them.

After the advice to keep the pilot away from battleships, some naval footage leads to Cleese at his desk with the tide coming in around him as he introduces the Batley Townswomen's Guild again, who are to follow up last year's re-enactment of Pearl harbour with their take on the first heart transplant. They begin fighting with handbags in the sea. Cleese, by now almost submerged, directs us to undersea presentations of *Measure For measure*, *Hello Dolly* and Formula Two Car Racing.

We then see Chapman and Cleese as two women listening to a dramatisation of 'The Death Of Mary Queen Of Scots' on the radio. They listen to the production, which largely consists of 'Are you Mary Queen of Scots?' in a broad Scottish accent followed by bangs and screams. Part Two immediately follows on another channel and consists of Mary announcing she isn't dead yet, with more bangs, screams and sawing noises. An announcement then

warns that BBC Radio 4 will now explode, and the radio blows up. They turn
to the television, which they are puzzled to see has a penguin on top of it.
After a discussion about the dangers of an egg rolling into the workings, the
announcer states that their penguin will blow up. It does.

The insanity is near to a close now, with Palin as Inspector Muffin The Mule
bursting into a room and telling a family (including Chapman in absurd sailor's
uniform) that there has been a murder, but he immediately corrects himself
and says it has actually been a Burnley, which he again corrects to burglary.
After a short while of this confusion, Sgt Duckie comes in with a squad of
policemen and performs 'Sgt Duckie's Song', the UK entry in the Europolice
Song Content. Idle as a Eurovision Girl announces the results and we hear
the winning entry, Inspector Zatapathique of the Monaco Murder Squad
performing 'Bing Tiddle Tiddle Bong' over the credits.

Comments.

In subsequent versions on record and on stage, the 'Bruces' sketch
would lead into the 'The Philosophers Song', but here it is ended with an
explanation of 'Sydney Nolan! What's that?' pointing at Cleese's ear. Sydney
Nolan was an Australian modern artist well known for his paintings of Ned
Kelly among other things.

Barry Humphries claimed at the time that the 'Bruces' idea had been stolen
from him, and a character he had by that name, but the writers Cleese and
Idle refuted this, claiming instead that the idea was simply born of the fact that
almost every Australian they knew seemed to be called Bruce.

The four soldiers in the front rank of the 'camp Military' sketch are actual
dancers hired for the episode (the Pythons are in the back row). These four are
Roy Gunson, Ralph Wood, Alexander Curry and Rod Clement. Of the four, for
some reason, only Clement is uncredited.

The police choir accompanying Sgt Duckie is again made up of the Fred
Tomlinson Singers, who also take part in the 'Bing Tiddle Tiddle Bong'
performance, which was written by Tomlinson and Chapman.

The bikini girls are uncredited, but they comprise: Flanagan (see other
episodes), Beulah Hughes (see future episodes), Marie (an erotic model of
the time), Benny Hill girl Barbara Lindley and Sandra Richards (see Episode
four in this series). Uncredited 'Naughty Bits' models were Karen Kerr, Nick
Moody, Malcolm Holbrooks and John Freeman. The Kamikaze pilot (named Mr
Kamikaze) is played by Vincent Wong, who also appeared in *Dr Who*.

The episode is notable for a rather ahead-of-it's-time joke announcing
'Margaret Thatcher's Brain' and pointing at her knee. At this point, she was
Education Secretary but almost a decade off becoming PM. Reginald Maudling
is mentioned once again, as he has been several times this series. He was
a Conservative politician (Home Secretary at the time) who had more than
a whiff of financial scandal about him, mercilessly seized upon by *Python*,
of course. He is also in the photo of Edward Heath's cabinet in one of the

Naughty Bits shots, as is Thatcher. There is also another mention (the third one) for 'Ann Hayden-Jones and her husband Pip', who are credited with dramatising the Death of Mary Queen Of Scots for radio.

In the sketch about the penguin on the TV, Chapman's exclamation of 'Intercourse the penguin!' was reportedly an ad-lib to avoid bleeping out a swear word. Cleese can be seen trying to stifle a laugh at this, as he also does at Chapman's suggestion that penguins come from Burma.

The character name 'Inspector Muffin The Mule' was included in the script but is not spoken nor included in a caption, so only the cast knew the name of the character.

Author's Pick.
A patchy episode, with several inspired short sections but nothing particularly lasting, the pick of the week, therefore, has to come down to a short scene of excellence. For that reason, the two candidates are the 'Cosmetic Surgery' sketch, for the climactic romp through the countryside and the 'Killer Cars' for the memorable sight of the cars pouncing from behind things. By a nose (pun absolutely intended) the cars win out over the proboscis, not least because they are one of the great *Python* animations to have stuck in the memory.

Episode Ten: Scott Of The Antarctic
First aired 1 December 1970
Sketches Include:
French Subtitled Film
Scott of the Antarctic
Scott of the Sahara
Conrad Poohs and His Dancing Teeth (Animation)
Fish Licence
Derby Council vs All Blacks Rugby Match
Long John Silver Impersonators v. Bournemouth Gynaecologists

Synopsis:
The opening scene this time out has Jones and Cleveland in an arty French subtitled film. She is sitting on a chair at a rubbish dump surrounded by seagulls, while he approaches her as a revolutionary sophisticate. They talk blandly for a while until Idle's TV cinema review host begins raving about it. We cut to another scene in which she is now holding a Webb's Wonder lettuce which, according to Idle, symbolises consumerism. It blows up, and Idle gushes admiration for the powerful message before introducing a new production in progress of *Scott Of The Antarctic* which is, unusually, being filmed in Paignton. Apart from the obvious problem that there is no snow on the beach, making the Devon resort a problematic location, another issue arises when a scene involving Scott fighting a lion has to be cut when Cleese's manic director discovers there are no lions in the Antarctic. An alternative

twenty-foot penguin with poisonous tentacles is considered before the decision is taken to change the film to 'Scott Of The Sahara', thereby using the sand. The lion fight takes place in two forms (stuffed and man in lion suit) before the twenty-foot penguin mysteriously also joins the fray.

This whole business has taken up seventeen and a half minutes of the allotted thirty when Cleese at his desk on the beach finally announces the credits, and we all await the remaining twelve minutes. This begins with a classic animated scene of 'Conrad Poohs and his Dancing Teeth', which is exactly what you think it will be. This follows with Cleese entering a Post Office following a lengthy backward animation gag, in the guise again of Mr Praline from the 'Parrot Sketch', whereupon he attempts to purchase a Fish License for his pet halibut, Eric. He refuses to believe that such a thing is not necessary, producing his supposed Cat License, which has 'dog' crossed out and 'cat' written in crayon. He demands a written statement from the mayor, who enters in the form of a ten-foot-tall Chapman surrounded by an entourage of Aldermen. He signs the exemption form before going off to play for Derby Council in the second half of a Rugby Union match against the New Zealand All Blacks. The council win, and we then see highlights of a rather one-sided football match between Bournemouth Gynaecologists and Watford Long John Silver Impersonators, which the Gynaecologists win easily owing to the fact that the Long John Silvers merely stand still with wooden legs and parrots, saying 'Aah! Jim Lad!' over and over again. We cut back to the studio announcer, Palin, who signs off with a very predictable joke before the old faithful 16-ton weight falls on his head.

Comments.

The French film, the 'Scott' features and the rugby and football encounters were all filmed in Devon in the same week in May when the fateful meeting between Cleese and rude hotelier Mr Sinclair happened. The former was at a Paignton rubbish dump, the second at Goodrington Sands, the rugby match at Torquay Rugby Ground and the football at Barton Fields, also in Torquay.

Carol Cleveland plays most of the female parts in this episode, but Eric Idle's then-wife Lyn Ashley makes a brief appearance, again credited as 'Mrs Idle'. Cleveland's part in 'Scott' proves to be easily her most seriously comedic role up to this point.

During the 'Fish Licence' sketch, Mr Praline makes outlandish claims about the pet-owning habits of several historical figures. These are as follows: Sir Gerald Nabaro (a prawn called Salmon) – UK politician and Transport Minister; Dawn Palethorpe (a clam called Stafford) – lady showjumper of the time; Alan Bullock (twp pikes, both called Chris) – a British historian who wrote the first comprehensive biography of Adolf Hitler; Marcel Proust (a haddock) – French novelist later to be immortalised in the *Python* annals in the 'Summarised Proust Competition'; Kemal Ataturk (an entire menagerie all called Abdul) – founder of the Republic of Turkey. Dawn Palethorpe also takes part in the Derby Council rugby match, we are informed. She is on horseback ('Sir Gerald'), playing on the wing.

The animation of Conrad Poohs (of the dancing teeth) is a photograph of Terry Gilliam.

Author's Picks.

Once again, this is a less than vintage episode, with long sections falling a little flat. The dancing teeth are a highlight, as is the 'Fish Licence' sketch, but I will vote for 'Scott Of The Sahara', if only for the lion. The earlier part, 'Scott Of The Antarctic' is overlong and struggles under its own weight.

Episode Eleven: How Not To Be Seen
First aired 8 December 1970
Sketches Include:
Conquistador Coffee Campaign
Exchange & Mart
Agatha Christie Sketch (railway timetables)
Film Director/Dentist Martin Curry (teeth)
Crackpot Religions Ltd
How Not to Be Seen
Interview in Filing Cabinet

Synopsis:

We open the show this time out with Cleese in a management company office, reading a book entitled 'Chinese For Advertising Men'. There is a knock on the door, and Mr S Frog (Idle) enters through the window. He is immediately berated by an unhappy Cleese for his ad campaign on behalf of Conquistador Coffer Ltd, explaining that the Conquistador chief is so unhappy he has shot himself. We learn that such decisions as rebranding the company as 'Conquistador Leprosy' and giving away a promotional free dead dog, have contributed to this. Frog argues that people know the name, which is countered by the claim that while this is true, they have burned down the factory. Just before the sketch begins to sag, we have a corny reveal that he is Cleese's son, then we cut to an idyllic coastal scene outside the window. The soaring music begins to stick and repeat, and we pan around to see Cleese as announcer moving the needle on an old gramophone. Continuing the joke, his 'Completely Different' announcement also sticks, as does the title sequence.

A frankly pointless short clip of Palin as Ramsay MacDonald entering 10 Downing Street and performing a full striptease, down to stockings and suspenders, cuts to a man behind a desk furtively viewing it on a projector. He (Cleese) is the editor of 'Exchange & Mart' magazine when Jones comes in for a job interview. The main joke here is that everything is offered as bartering to be bought and sold, and we soon move onto an animation showing his secretary swamped by an invasion of Chinese Communists and from there into another of the *Python* period-film Agatha Christie parodies. This time the joke revolves around all parties talking in fascinated detail about railway timetables, and the motive for the murder is revealed to be the prize of a prime reserved seat. It could easily fail, but it is so skillfully executed, that it manages to be very funny indeed. We learn that the writer was an obsessed railway enthusiast named Neville Shunt, who is enthusiastically lauded as a genius by critic Gavin Millarrrrr (Cleese).

After another rather laboured routine with Chapman as a film director with two enormous (six inches long) front teeth, showing clips of his work, all of which feature characters with increasingly enormous front incisors, we are into the 'Crackpot Religions' sketch, poking fun at the idea of organised religion together with a parody of then-new game show *Sale Of The Century*. A woman chooses a hymn number, and the curtain goes back to reveal that she has won 'the entire Norwich City Council'. The sketch goes on to poke fun at such easy targets as Catholics, drunken Australians, lunatics, John Lennon and corrupt priests involved in organised crime. There are guest appearances for previous *Python* faces in the shape of Archbishop Nudge, Archbishop Gumby and Archbishop Shabby.

The following scene is the title piece, 'How Not To Be Seen', an outside shot of people hiding, and getting blown up when they reveal themselves, and ultimately even when they wise up and keep hiding. It's fun but too long, and the episode rather peters out with an interview with a footballer who is inside a filing cabinet and finally an appearance from Jackie Charlton and the Tonettes performing 'Yummy Yummy Yummy' from within large packing crates. A thirty-second sequence of clips from the show at speed is then shown for those who missed it.

Comments.
An animated scene was cut out of all UK showings of the 'Crackpot Religions' sketch. It featured a workman repairing a telegraph pole which turns out to be one of three crucifixes with Christ in the centre of the three men, while signposts advertise the availability of the Prince Of Darkness. While it was removed, it was left in the quick recap at the end, and pausing at the right time will reveal a brilliant still of the crosses.

The critic 'Gavin Millarrrrr' is a parody of actual Scottish director and film critic Gavin Millar. Similarly, the 'Jackie Charlton' referred to in the music scene at the end is the footballing brother of Bobby Charlton, both of whom played for England in the 1966 World Cup win.

The 'How Not To Be Seen' sketch was most probably inspired by Spike Milligan's similar routine in which the National Anthem is played to see how many hiding people will stand up. All who do are blown up.

Making an uncredited appearance in this episode, as one of the Norwich City Council and also the body in the Agatha Christie sketch, is Lewis Alexander. A veteran of some 110 film and TV roles (largely small in nature), he lived until 2010, when he passed away at the age of 100.

During Cleese's breathless appraisal of Neville Shunt's work, he delivers the line 'The point is taken, the elk is dead, the beast stops at Swindon, Chabrol stops at nothing.' Claude Chabrol was a contentious French film director known for breaking taboos and, indeed, supposedly stopping at nothing.

Author's Pick.
This is not a great episode overall, full of weak ideas and sketches which seem promising but do not work. The two clear front-runners here are the 'Conquistador Coffee' sketch and the Agatha Christie 'Railway Timetable', but I will give it by a whisker to the coffee campaign.

Episode Twelve: Spam
First aired 15 December 1970
Sketches Include:
The Black Eagle
Hungarian Phrasebook
Court (phrasebook)
Ypres 1914 (abandoned)]
Art Gallery Strikes
Ypres 1914
Hospital for Over-Actors
Gumby Flower Arranging
Spam

Synopsis:
The beginning of this episode takes the 'false opening' motif to new heights, as 'The Black Eagle' is an entirely authentic-looking historical film, complete with grandiose captioning ('... the Spanish empire lay in ruins...') and even page after page of credits with no obvious joke to be seen. After these credits, we see a small boat approach a beach, carrying some men who seem to have no *Python* connection. We only realise what is going on when they proceed across the beach to reveal Cleese sat at his desk for the usual opening. This is two and a half minutes into the show, so we can only surmise at the number of people when the show was first broadcast who must have been frantically changing the channel, believing themselves to be on the wrong one. Only *Monty Python* would attempt to fool their own audience into thinking they weren't on and switching off!

After the opening titles, we are into a Tobacconists shop, with a caption tying in to the beginning (1970, and the British empire lay in ruins... etc) before Cleese enters as a Hungarian tourist with a wholly erroneous phrasebook, causing him to ask for a box of matches with 'My hovercraft is full of eels' and follow that up with 'Do you want to come to my place, bouncy bouncy'.

The shopkeeper borrows the book to find the phrase for 'that's six shillings and sixpence please', but when he reads it out he is punched in the face. A policeman (Chapman) hears this punch from several streets away and comes running, only to be greeted with 'Drop your panties Sir William, I cannot wait until lunchtime', and the hapless Hungarian is arrested.

Next up we are in a courtroom where publisher Palin is on trial for distributing the offending phrasebook. This moves quickly on to a TV Show called 'World Forum', which features guests Karl Marx, Mao Tse-Tung, Lenin and Che Guevara competing in a quiz show which seems to centre around music and sport. Mao Tse-Tung demonstrates unexpected knowledge of the 1959 Eurovision Song Contest while Marx begins well in his quest to win a three-piece lounge suite with two correct answers on Communism before being undone by a question regarding the 1949 FA Cup Final.

It's a World War One sketch next, which is quickly abandoned owing to extraneous people hanging about in the scenery, and we cut to an art gallery where characters are going missing from paintings and taking strike action for consultation with regard to where they hang. After continuing this theme through an animated sequence, we are back to the 'Ypres 1914' scene, in which lots have to be drawn to decide who will stay behind, owing to a lack of rations, and take their own lives. Chapman is the officer outranking them, who is chosen to stay as he has of drawn the short straw, even after he insists it is redone twice. He even loses at a game of 'you're it' and then 'rock paper scissors', before eventually claiming that the heroic, armless Padre must go as he didn't enter a hand. The Padre, at this point, embarks on an impassioned rant which results in him being rushed by ambulance to the Hospital for Over Actors, which is crammed with frantically gurning Long John Silvers and Richard The Thirds. A short but very amusing 'Gumby Flower Arranging' demonstration follows this.

Closing the show is the short but immortal 'Spam' which, of course, centres around a small cafe which sells almost entirely Spam-based dishes. A group of Vikings are seated at a table and quickly begin to overpower things with the famous 'Spam Song'. Finally, the end credits insert the word Spam into everybody's name – even the production staff!

Comments.
The Tobacconist's shop where the 'Hungarian Phrase Book' sketch takes place is the same building (Pickford's Newsagent as was) from which Cleese began the 'Silly Walks' sketch. The terraced street where Chapman runs along toward the shop looks very much like the same one that all of the gas men queued up in for the 'New Cooker' sketch'.

Unusually (particularly of late) there are no female parts in this episode whatsoever. An episode with no part for Cleveland is a rarity at this point. The man playing Mao Tse-Tung in the 'World Forum' sketch looks a little like Neil Innes making his debut *Python* appearance at a glance, but it is, in fact, an uncredited appearance by actor Basil Tang.

The 'Hungarian' phrase which gets the Tobacconist punched in the face is in fact meaningless. It was apparently gibberish made up to 'sound foreign'. The DVD release of the episode contains a deliberate subtitling error during the 'Spam' sketch. When Cleese's Hungarian reappears in that scene and tries to order food, his words are 'My lower intestine is full of Spam, Egg, Spam, Bacon, Spam, Tomatoes, Spam.' However the subtitles read 'Your intestine is full of sperm'!

The use of the word 'Spam' to mean unwanted marketing electronic mail is supposedly directly derived from the 'Spam' sketch.

In the opening credits for the fake movie, 'The Black Eagle', the character of 'Second Wench' is credited to Tinea Pedis, which is the medical term for athlete's foot.

Author's Pick.

This episode contains two *Python* 'big-hitters' in the shape of 'Spam' and 'Hungarian Phrase Book', but despite the brilliance of Cleese's Hungarian in particular, I will buck the trend once more and plump for 'Ypres 1914', if only for Chapman's superb portrayal of the cowardly officer fighting desperately to portray the claim that rank plays no part. Masterful.

Episode Thirteen: Royal Episode 13

First aired 22 December 1970
Sketches Include:
Coal Mine
The Man Who Says Things in a Very Roundabout Way
Commercials
How to Feed a Goldfish
The Man Who Collects Birdwatcher's Eggs
Insurance Sketch
Hospital Run by RSM
Exploding Version of "The Blue Danube"
Girls Boarding School
Submarine
Lifeboat
Undertakers sketch

Synopsis:
The opening of this final episode of the second series is very different from the norm, even by *Python* standards. Eschewing the regular 'And now' or 'It's', Cleese informs us in very serious tones that the Queen will be watching part of the show. However, which part or for how long is unknown. The opening title sequence is very regal and entirely different, with the music changed to 'Land of Hope and Glory'. As the first sketch begins, showing Welsh coal

Above: The Pythons, probably not pictured enjoying a joke... L-R Jones, Chapman, Cleese, Idle, Gilliam, Palin. (*BBC*)

Below: Michael Palin with the 'Seventh Python', the lovely Carol Cleveland, on the set of *Holy Grail.* *(Sony)*

Left: 'I bet she does, I bet she does...' From the first *Flying Circus* series, the classic 'Nudge Nudge' sketch with Idle and Jones. (*BBC*)

Right: Yes, you knew we'd have to have a photo of it! It's none other than 'The Dead Parrot Sketch'. Insert your favourite quote. (*BBC*)

Left: 'Marriage Guidance Counsellor'. Things are about to go very, very wrong for Arthur Pewtey. Idle, Palin, Cleveland. (*BBC*)

Right: 'Screw! Bend! Inflate! Alter Saddle!' It's 'Bicycle Repair Man' (Palin). (*BBC*)

Left: 'Aye, 'ampstead wasn't good enough for you, was it? You had to go poncing off to Barnsley, you and yer coal-mining friends'. Graham Chapman in the brilliant 'Working Class Playwright'. (*BBC*)

Right: A typically surreal, and frankly alarming, Terry Gilliam image from the first series. (*BBC*)

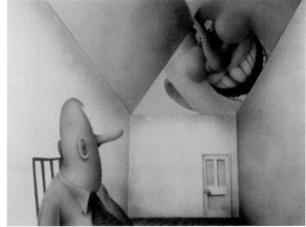

Left: It's not the most unusual place Cleese's desk has ended up, but it's getting there. This became a familiar link during Series Two. (*BBC*)

Right: All together now: '*Nobody* expects the Spanish Inquisition!!' Now, what were their chief weapons again? (Jones, Palin, Gilliam). (*BBC*)

Left: Carol Cleveland getting all dramatic in the quite inspired 'Semaphore Version Of *Wuthering Heights*'. (*BBC*)

Right: Series Three brought us the somewhat less than idyllic retreat of Whicker Island. Alan 'John Cleese' Whicker in the foreground. (*BBC*)

Left: '... until the word 'Maudling' is almost totally obscured'. BBC newsreader Richard Baker making a guest appearance in Series Three. (*BBC*)

Right: 'All brontosauruses are thin at one end, much MUCH thicker in the middle, and then thin again at the far end. That is the theory that I have'. John Cleese in astonishing 'Anne Elk' make-up with Chapman. (*BBC*)

Left: 'The Cycing Tour'. Ken Pither is invited by three quite normal men, who are not Secret Police at all, to a 'Clambake'. Chapman, Idle, Cleese, Palin. (*BBC*)

Right: 'Silhouetted against the crim ... crim ... crimisy ... crimson! against the crimson stray ... stree ... Streaked!'. 'A Book At Bedtime', struggling with Sir Walter Scott's *Redgauntlet*. (*BBC*)

Left: Gilliam's artwork for 'The Golden Age Of Ballooning'. All bets were off as regards what show introduction we would get by the time of Series Four. (*BBC*)

Right: Mrs Elizabeth III and Mrs Mock-Tudor, with bizarre 'TV Remote Servant' in 'The Public Are Idiots' sketch. Chapman, Jones and an astonishing Gilliam. (*BBC*)

Left: It's *Nationwide*. Eric Idle in front of a background graphic which will be instantly familiar to anyone in the UK of a certain age. (*BBC*)

Right: It's not over until the fat man sings, to paraphrase a saying. A somewhat appropriate Gilliam image from the final series. (*BBC*)

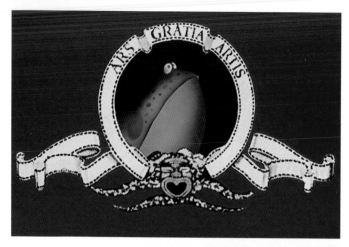

Left: Introducing 'Conrad Poohs And His Dancing Teeth' in the film *And Now For Something Completely Different* – yes, it's 20th Century Frog! (*Sony*)

Right: 'With my best girl by my side...' Palin with Connie Booth in the film version of 'Lumberjack Song'. (*Sony*)

Left: 'Now they're under starter's orders ... and they're off! Ah no, they're not. No they didn't realise they were supposed to start'. 'Upper Class Twit Of The Year' revisited for *And Now For Something Completely Different*. (*Sony*)

Right: The second album *Another Monty Python Record*. Nothing to do with Beethoven, whose tennis career was examined on the back cover. *(Universal)*

Left: The third album, *Monty Python's Previous Record*, complete with quintessentially 'Pythonesque' cover art by Terry Gilliam. *(Universal)*

Right: The *Monty Python Matching Tie And Handkerchief* album. This is the original UK release; the US cover has the tie and handkerchief displayed in a different 'display box', though still with the same infamous insert. *(Universal)*

Left: The original UK *Monty Python Instant Record Collection*, which assembled into a large box which resembled a record collection. See Appendix. *(Universal)*

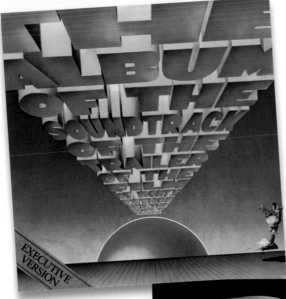

Left: *The Album Of The Soundtrack Of The Trailer Of The Film...* The glorious cover art for the excellent *Holy Grail* soundtrack album. *(Universal)*

Right: The *Holy Grail* opening credits: 'Sir Not-Appearing-In-This-Film'. It's Michael Palin's infant son William – or as he now prefers to be known, Director of Conservation at the Old Royal Naval College, Greenwich. I'm sure he's not embarrassed. *(Sony)*

Left: 'We're Knights of the Round Table, We dance when e'er we're able' – On second thoughts, let us not go to Camelot. It is a silly place. *(Sony)*

Right: Gilliam's striking God animation from *Holy Grail*, based on a photograph of Victorian English cricketer Dr W G Grace. (*Sony*)

Left: King Arthur with his brave knights. Well, with his knights, anyway. Palin as Sir Galahad and Jones as Sir Bedevere. (*Sony*)

Right: 'Your mother was a hamster and your father smelt of elderberries!' Cleese as the legendary French Taunter, who mercilessly taunts the knights on two occasions from his battlements'. (*Sony*)

Left: The Three Wise Men appear at the crib of Brian. And soon leave when they find out that the Messiah is next door. It's actually (L-R) Cleese, Chapman, Palin. (*Sony*)

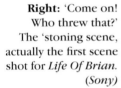

Right: 'Come on! Who threw that?' The 'stoning scene, actually the first scene shot for *Life Of Brian.* (*Sony*)

Left: The People's Front Of Judea: Idle, Cleese, Palin, Sue Jones-Davis. What had the Romans ever done for them? (*Sony*)

Right: 'The Messiah! Show us the Messiah!' The crowd outside Brian's window. 'He's not the Messiah, he's a very naughty boy'. (*Sony*)

Left: 'We've got lumps of it round the back'. Eric Idle and the astonishingly made-up Gilliam as the Jailer and his assistant. (*Sony*)

Right: 'You come from nothing. You're going back to nothing. What have you lost? Nothing!' Come on, join in the chorus... (*Sony*)

Left: Terry Gilliam's latest take on The Almighty, from *The Meaning Of Life*. (*Sony*)

Right: 'I've given this long and careful thought, and it has to be medical experiments for the lot of you'. The classic 'Every Sperm Is Sacred' scene from *The Meaning Of Life*. (*Sony*)

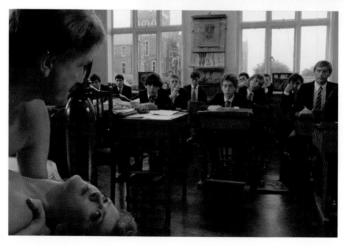

Left: 'Oh, do pay attention, Wadsworth! I know it's Friday afternoon..' John Cleese and the 'Sex Education Class'. (*Sony*)

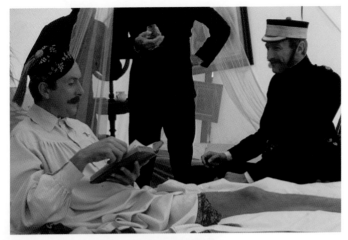

Right: 'Complete mystery to me. Woke up just now, one sock too many'. Eric Idle, taking a leg being bitten off on the chin. (*Sony*)

Left: 'One more wafer-theen mint? They are wafer-theen...' Mr Creosote, prior to his unfortunate mint-related explosion. (*Sony*)

Right: 'The Salmon Mousse!!' The Grim Reaper explains his presence as we bid the *Python* films farewell. (*Sony*)

Left: 'You were lucky!' The immortal 'Four Yorkshiremen' sketch, from *Monty Python Live (Mostly)*, 2014. *(Eagle Rock)*

Right: 'Michaelangelo And The Pope', from the sometimes funny, sometimes slightly sad final reunion for *Monty Python Live (Mosty)*. *(Eagle Rock)*

Left: Let's give the last word to Mr Cleese... from *Monty Python Live At The Hollywood Bowl* – 'ALBATROSS!!' *(Sony)*

miners fighting among themselves concerning the veracity of various historical minutiae, a caption informs us the Her Majesty is 'still watching *The Virginian*'.

We then cut to a TV programme entitled 'The Toad Elevating Moment', in which the first guest we see is a man who speaks in a very roundabout way. He answers in single words because he doesn't feel very talkative. Following him are three men who, respectively, say only the beginnings, middles and ends of words, and things run out of steam rather quickly. We head to an advertising break, with an animated toothpaste advert showing a ravenous dragon driving away its damsel victims with bad breath being followed by live-action commercials for washing powder and surgical appliances.

Idle comes onto our screens next, with his advice about how to feed a goldfish quickly unravelling when he pours gazpacho soup into the bowl, closely followed by sausages, veg and sauté potatoes which he is still cramming in when he gets carried off. Jones is up next, as Herbert Mental, a man who sneaks up on birdwatchers and steals their eggs from their packed lunches for his collection. This goes into a routine about the sport of pigeon-fancier racing. The following 'Insurance Sketch', concerning a requirement for the client to produce a twelve-gallon urine sample just to prove he is serious about insurance, is merely a vehicle for the announcement that Her Majesty has tuned in. Both men and the studio audience stand to attention as Idle (the client) prepares to tell 'the first royal joke of the evening. Unfortunately we then get the news that she has 'switched over to *News At Ten*', amid groans. We are then treated to a sublime moment in which we see newsreader Reginald Bosanquet, the actual regular newsman from ITV's *News At Ten* programme, who is reading a story when the National Anthem begins playing, and he stands to attention, still reading. This was a unique moment for the time, as rival channels BBC and ITV hardly even admitted to each others' existence, let alone make an appearance on the other side in this way.

From this we go to an exterior-based sketch involving a hospital run along the lines of an Army barracks, with a regimental Sergeant Major drilling lines of patients bandaged practically head to toe, followed by cross country running for the more severely ill. This leads us into the 'Exploding Blue Danube', in which a small orchestra in a field plays the 'Blue Danube Waltz, with sections being periodically blown up until only the conductor remains. Next is an utterly surreal 'Girl's Public School dormitory', where, in total, darkness we hear several very butch voices purporting to be said girls, until the light goes on and Miss Rogers (Cleveland) enters, causing several men in string vests and schoolgirl uniforms to get back into bed and, oddly, two large pantomime geese to flee the scene. Most bizarrely of all, in lieu of a chandelier, a goat hangs suspended from the ceiling, with an illuminated light-bulb at the end of each hoof.

We discover that this was, in fact, 'The Naughtiest Girl In School', starring the men of the 14th Marine Commandos, and it is followed up by 'The Normandy beach landing, performed by the girls of Oakdene High School, Upper Fifth

Science'. In other words, film of the landings with a voiceover of squealing girls' voices. This leads, thematically, to a submarine, manned by Jones, Chapman and Palin in the guises of the old ladies, or 'Pepperpots' as they were generally known, as they end up firing Mrs Nesbitt out of the torpedo tube, where she was resting with a headache.

This leads us into the finale of the show and the series, in the shape of the two 'cannibalism' sketches. First, we see a lifeboat with our five heroes aboard, starving after 33 days adrift. Talk turns to staying alive and the Captain, Cleese, struggling with a 'gammy leg', offers himself to be eaten. This gets a mixed reaction owing to his leg, and much to his wounded pride, they express a desire to eat Johnson (Jones) instead. Amid people becoming offended at not being appetising, a plan is drawn up to eat selected parts from each of them, and a waitress appears to take their order. This is followed up with a spectacularly offensive 'cannibalism' animated scene, an offended letter, a man with a stoat through his head and finally the uber-offensive 'Undertakers Sketch', in which Cleese turns up at an undertaker with his deceased mother in a bag. With the first suggestion of dumping her in the Thames not popular, undertaker Chapman suggests eating her ('cooked. Not raw...'), and when a 'peckish' Cleese is unsure, it is decided to eat her and then dig a grave where, if he feels guilty, he can throw up in afterwards. The sketch is accompanied, and often drowned out, by the disgusted 'audience' booing and then rushing the stage. As a result, much of its effect is lost.

Comments.
As well as having a disgusted audience reaction added to it (part of a BBC ruling to allow the sketch to go ahead), the 'Undertaker Sketch' was deleted in many screenings. It was later reinserted from a copy of a US tape, which explains the poorer film quality of the sketch in some versions of the show. It was re-recorded without interruptions for the second *Python* record album and is much the better for it. Note that the producer, Ian McNaughton, was in the audience at the front as a 'plant', to lead them in the set invasion.

The two men in the 'Insurance Sketch' are named Mr Martin and Mr Feldman, in homage to Marty Feldman.

The animation directly following the 'Pigeon Fanciers' Race features another guest appearance from Spiny Norman, looming over St Martin-In-The-Fields and shouting 'Dinsdale!'

In the submarine, it is clear that Palin is pretending to knit, while Jones, on the other hand, is actually knitting properly.

The Virginian, which it is reported that the Queen is watching when the show begins, was a Western TV programme which ran from 1962 to 1971.

Talking about his collection of birdwatchers' eggs, Jones expresses his desire to be featured on the regional section of *Nationwide*, which was, in fact, a UK current affairs show broadcast at 6 pm each weekday from 1969 until 1983. The show would contain a segment where each region would show local items in their area. These sections had names such as *Look North, Midlands Today* and *Reporting Scotland*. The programme would be parodied further in a later *Python* episode.

In a bizarre twist of parodic fate, the Crelm toothpaste advert showing the dragon unable to get damsels to eat because of his bad breath inspired a real-life advertising campaign for Listerine Antiseptic Mouthwash, which featured actor and comedian Willy Rushton voicing the smoking-and-drinking dragon.

The fake TV programme in the episode, 'The Toad Elevating Moment' was one of the possible planned titles for the show.

Author's Pick.
This is another episode which has some brilliant ideas which are not quite done justice to. The hospital and coal mine sketches have seeds of hilarity buried in them, while the running pigeon-fanciers, speeded up with wildly flapping arms, are extremely funny, if short. The climactic undertaker routine is entirely ruined by the BBC's insistence on the ridiculous audience heckling. Overall, I would give the award to the 'Lifeboat' sketch, which at least retains its offensive purpose.

Series Three
All episodes produced and directed by Ian MacNaughton

Things were starting to develop and evolve in the *Python* world by this point, and the dynamic was beginning to alter. Michael Palin has said that by this time Cleese and Idle had begun to view *Python* as a step toward other things, while at the other end of the scale Terry Jones simply adored the work for its own sake. He saw himself and Chapman as occupying the middle ground. What is certain is that Chapman's drinking, which had been heavy from the beginning, was starting to become more of an issue, while Cleese was beginning to grow cold to the idea of more TV shows.

In the event, of course, Cleese did sign up for this third series, though he would be gone by the truncated fourth. There was a year's gap between Series Two in 1970 and Series Three in 1972, as 1971 was filled by other *Python* activity. They began, early in the year, to develop the show into a stage performance, with an initial low-key - if rapturously received - performance in Coventry spawning bigger and grander settings. A year later, in 1972, they would appear at the Isle Of Wight Festival, going on just before the Beach Boys, to 50,000 people. The first feature film, *And Now For Something Completely Different* was released, and there were a pair of shows recorded in German, bizarrely enough, titled *Monty Python's Fliegender Zirkus*, for German TV and filmed on location in Bavaria.

A *Monty Python* compilation show was entered into the prestigious 'Golden Rose Of Montreux' festival in 1971, where, ironically, it was beaten by an Austrian *Python* homage entitled *Peter Lodynski's Flea-Market Company*.

Episode One: Whicker's World
First aired 19 October 1972
Sketches include:
Njorl's Saga 1
Multiple Murderer Court Scene
Investigating the body
Njorl's Saga 2
Eric Njorl Court Scene
Stock Exchange Report
Mrs. Premise and Mrs. Conclusion
Whicker's World

Synopsis:
After a false start with 'Njorl's Saga', an epic Icelandic tale from 1126, which sees the hero unable to get on his horse, we go to a courtroom where Eric Idle is the accused, while the Judge (Jones) reads out the full charge of the murder of twenty people, including Lord and Lady Kimberley of Pretoria, in one morning. Idle addresses the court, and delivers a heartfelt string of apologies,

not so much to the victims but certainly to the court, the police (swathed in bandages) and the jury for wasting their valuable time. Despite begging for a heavy sentence, he eventually gets six months suspended and a rousing chorus of 'For He's A Jolly Good Fellow'. This leads us to a bizarre animated search for a criminal who has escaped into his own body. The police follow him through various organs and veins, complete with ornate staircases and the general appearance of a mansion. It's brilliantly done.

It is then back to Njorl, who is still failing to get onto his horse. An announcer, Cleese, informs us that he has been in touch with the North Malden Icelandic Saga Society, who will assist. Lo and behold, he mounts the beast and, after riding twelve days and nights without rest, finally reaches his goal. This is shown as a sign reading 'North Malden – Please Drive Carefully'. He rides down the high street as we are informed of the marvellous amenities in this promised land, and as we are treated to a lengthy hymn of praise to the town by the mayor, a voice-over interjects with an apology of the material not being quite close enough to the theme of Twelfth-Century Iceland. We hear Cleese on the phone to the North Malden Icelandic Saga Society, who promise they will tone it down. Sure enough, he rides away back into the wilds where he stops by a river and meets six armoured knights, who reveal their shields bearing the letters MALDEN, and as they begin fighting, signs praising the wonders of North Malden are waved aloft.

It's back to the courtroom now where a man merely giving evidence regarding BBC programme scheduling becomes indignant and is hauled off and given five years, in contrast to the charming mass murderer. Eric Njorl, head to foot in bandages like a mummy, is in the dock, accused of 'Publicising a London Borough in the course of a BBC saga'. A policeman, Constable Pan-Am, is brought in and goes berserk with his truncheon, beating the unfortunate Njorl then rounding on everyone in range, including the other police. He gives evidence, and it then becomes obvious that Njorl is standing stock still. This is investigated, and the bandages are empty, leading to another animation followed by a short but amusing Stock market Report. A further animation ends with an old woman entering a laundrette, where we see Cleese and Chapman as Mrs Premise and Mrs Conclusion, who talk nonsense for a while before they get onto the subject of Jean-Paul Sartre, who Mrs Premise met on holiday. They find a Paris phone book, phone him, and set off to visit. We see them on a raft near what they think is France before we see a sign reading North Malden. They sail on, as Idle delivers a speech in the guise of TV interviewer Alan Whicker extolling Malden's praises.

After a brief stop off in Iceland, the women reach Paris and find the Sartres, where Mrs Sartre complains that the place would be overrun with pamphlets if it weren't for the goat. We see the goat eating pamphlets. Finally, they see Sartre himself, who agrees with Mrs Premise's interpretation of his work, and they go home. This leads into the final sketch, the classic 'Whicker's World', where we see Whicker's Island, a place populated by 'ex-international interviewers', as the various *Python* boys repeatedly criss-cross past each other in the guise of Whicker, explaining about the island into their microphones. A resort shows one of the Whickers interviewing the only non-Whicker still in residence, Father Pierre, who says he stays there 'mainly for the interviews'. It's masterfully done.

Comments.

There are lots of guest stars in this one, but no Carol Cleveland. There are female speaking roles, in the shape of the first three members of the jury, who are all women with moustaches, but these are played by Lyn Ashley, Connie Booth and Rita Ashley. In an unusual move, there is a high profile guest star in a quite major role, namely Frank Williams, who was at the time very well known for his role as the vicar in *Dad's Army*. He plays the clerk of the court.

To today's audience, Alan Whicker may need some explaining. He was a very familiar TV presenter and interviewer, who fronted the TV show *Whicker's World* for over 30 years, during which time he travelled to most corners of the world, and interviewed many of the world's most famous and notorious people. The credits at the end of this episode have everyone listed with the word 'Whicker' somewhere in their names.

Palin can be seen trying not to laugh during his 'Constable Pan-Am' scene. This is because at that moment the mummified Njorl (a dummy by that time) had topped off its rostrum and was being hastily repositioned by floor staff.

Authors Pick.

This is another episode which has a number of ups and downs. There are very funny moments (Idle's charming murderer, Palin's psychotic Constable Pan-Am, some of the New Malden jokes), but the routine with Mrs Premise and Mrs Conclusion goes on way too long and ends up with its best jokes wasted as it becomes mildly irritating. Also there is a little too much in the courtroom. Overall, there can be only one winner here: the sublime 'Whicker's World' sketch. Everything here, from the performances to the direction (as they repeatedly cross paths) to the perfect parodying of Whicker's style in the writing, hits the mark completely, and it is, unlike other scenes, masterfully concise.

Episode Two: Mr And Mrs Brian Norris' Ford Popular

First aired 26 October 1972
Sketches include:
Emigration from Surbiton to Hounslow
Schoolboys' Life Assurance Company
How to Do It
Mrs Niggerbaiter Explodes
Farming Club
Trim-Jeans Theatre
The Fish-Slapping Dance

Titanic Sinking
The BBC is Short of Money
It's Man Show

Synopsis:
This classic episode opens with dramatic music accompanying the captions 'Kon-Tiki', 'Ra' and 'Ra 2' before concluding with 'Mr And Mrs Brian Norris' Ford Popular', as an old leather-bound tome is opened. We learn of the heroic expedition of Brian Norris and his wife (Palin and Chapman) from Surbiton to Hounslow, to prove his theory that the similarities between the two cultures indicate that there was a long-ago trek North to Hounslow by the natives of Surbiton. After months of planning they set out on the drive north, discovering along the way that boarding the 4:37 train to Hounslow provides the clue as to how the Thames may have been traversed. It's magnificent stuff.

The credits (with a naked Jones at a keyboard) then lead into a headmaster's office, with Head Palin summoning in three schoolboys. He berates these massively over-achieving youths for recklessly running a unit-trust linked assurance scheme with fringe benefits and full cash-in endowment facilities, without authorisation. He reveals that his wife his having trouble with her 'waterworks', and asks Jones, who is a surgeon, to assist. He protests that Stebbins (Idle) would be better placed as he is a gynaecologist, prompting an exclamation of 'Ooh, you rotten stinker, Tidwell!'

This leads into the credits for a Blue Peter parody 'How To Do It', with the genial hosts Alan, Noel and Jackie (Cleese, Chapman and Idle as perfect 'Pete, John and Val' clones) announcing that they will give the viewers tips on how to do things, such as 'how to irrigate the Sahara Desert and make vast new areas of land cultivatable' and Jackie's priceless explanation of 'how to rid the world of all known diseases'. It's possibly the most accurate and successful parody the team ever attempted, but it is kept concise for fear of overplaying the joke (in contrast to last week's laboured structuring). Instead, we go straight to a house where two 'pepperpot' women, Mrs Shazam and the absurdly named 'Mrs Nigger-Baiter', are talking as Mrs Shazam's son (Cleese) enters. He is an adult in city dress, but they both poke and prod him with baby talk, with the line 'Does he talk, eh?' answered with the deadpan 'Of course I can talk. I'm Minister for Overseas Development'. As he asks for a cup of tea before preparing a statement on Rhodesia for the Commons, there is a loud explosion, and there is much lamentation that 'Mrs N' has exploded, though this is dismissed as nothing unusual. A slight digression as Idle arrives at the door as a vicar selling things from a suitcase before we cut to a medical discussion about explosions, courtesy of Chapman. He is treating athlete's foot with TNT between each toe and admits to a record of 'eighty-four dead, sixty-five severely wounded and twelve missing believed cured,' before an animated sequence leads us to 'farming Club', a programme about agriculture presenting the life of Tchaikovsky.

By way of a brilliant physical comedy routine of an escapologist (Jones) playing Tchaikovsky's First Piano Concerto while escaping from a chained sack, we are into 'Trim-Jeans Theatre', in which people wearing absurd inflatable slimming aids in the form of shorts perform various dramatic roles. This takes us into the short, but immortal, 'Fish-Slapping Dance', in which Palin and Cleese, in khaki jackets and shorts on a dock, perform a sort of Morris Dance with fish. Palin prances forward several times with two small pilchards, slapping Cleese each time on both cheeks before the latter produces an enormous trout and knocks him immediately into the water. An animation then has his body eaten by a large German fish, complete with swastika, which is in turn eaten by a larger British fish, before that is itself eaten by an enormous Chinese fish, which proceeds to bite a large hole in the hull of the Titanic.

We see several crew members on the bridge of the stricken ship, at first attempting to dress up as woman and children, in order to fit into the 'Women and children first' directive, but as costumes run out are left with 'Women, children, red Indians, spacemen and sort of idealised versions of renaissance men first'. Miraculously, they survive, and we see them a few days later, captured for some unfathomable geographic reason by South American guards. While they are being interrogated, we learn of severe BBC financial issues, as extras speak by accident, costing money each time, and other added extras are performed such as stunts, camera effects and a pantomime routine from Puss In Boots. Idle, as a BBC announcer shivering naked in a bathroom, denies rumours of problems before we cut back to find the guards have sold their trousers to raise funds. We discover that they are in Venezuela, and the sailors are now from the SS Mother Goose, which was off Port Of Spain. During an inspirational monologue from Jones to this effect, the scenery is removed by men in overcoats, and they are revealed to be filming in someone's flat. They are initially told to leave as the *Horse Of The Year Show* is filming there, but we discover that is in the kitchen.

Finally, after the credits are shown on discarded bits of scrap paper, we see an extra – a chat show presented by the 'It's' man. Ringo Starr and Lulu are seated on large sofas. Our hero enters, sits down but utters the keyword 'It's' and triggers the *Python* music and titles in the background. The guests walk off, with Starr getting into a brawl with the 'It's' man in a truly surreal send-off.

Comments.

The two female characters this week (the escapologist's assistant and 'Puss In Boots'), are both played by Julia Breck, seen in a number of TV comedy roles up until 1982.

In the *Horse Of The Year Show* scene, with the showjumping demolishing the kitchen, Jones emerges from a cupboard wearing a large nose announcing 'It's one of our most popular programmes', before being turfed out and referred to as 'Mr Fox' Also Brian Norris can be seen reading a book entitled 'The Lady With The Naked Skin' by Paul Fox Jnr. Paul Fox was, in fact, the BBC Controller between 1967 and 1973. Note also in the Brian Norris sketch that we are told he is the author of 'A Short History of Motor Traffic Between Purley and Esher', but when we see this book in a shop window it is actually 'Esher and Purley'.

It is very likely that the business with the *Horse Of The Year Show* was a dig at the BBC postponing *Python* for two weeks in the second series in order to accommodate it.

The 'How To Do It' sketch parodied *Blue Peter*, a UK children's show which is an institution, running from the 1950s non-stop to the present day. The current presenters at the time of broadcast in 1972 were John Noakes, Peter Purves and Valerie Singleton, who are clearly caricatured here. The large dog is in reference to Petra, the *Blue Peter* dog at the time.

Sections of this episode indicate the changing standards in comedy and language within a few decades, as the name of the exploding woman would never be used today, while the description of Tchaikovsky as 'an old poof who wrote tunes' and the speech and appearance of the Chinese fish would similarly not make the cut. It is obvious from context, however, that this is in no way intended to offend, and hence is still screened today.

The Fish-Slapping Dance was filmed at Teddington Lock in London. Palin has said that during rehearsals the water level was high, but when the actual filming was done it had lowered significantly, hence his high and alarming dive into the water. This scene was a favourite of huge *Python* fan George Harrison and was listed as one of his favourite sketches. Note that it was originally recorded in 1971 for a pan-European May Day special titled *Euroshow 71*, then added into this episode a year later.

The final 'It's Man Chat Show' script originally called for 'four incredibly famous guests', and the Pythons were reportedly desperate to try to engineer the first Beatles reunion on TV. Attempts to lure John and Yoko ultimately failed, but Chapman had become friendly with Ringo on his film *The Magic Christian*, so the day was, more or less, saved!

Author's Pick.
This is very difficult to choose, as virtually everything in this sublime episode hits the mark. Any other week, 'Brian Norris', the over-achieving pupils or the 'Fish Slapping Dance' would have been almost guaranteed as the highlight, but I have to give it to the *Blue Peter* parody – though that is coloured by the fact that I was eleven years old at the time and an avid viewer of the children's programme.

Episode Three: The Money Programme
First aired 2 November 1972
Sketches include:
The Money Programme
Fraud Film Director Squad
Dead Bishop

Jungle Restaurant
The Argument Sketch
Hitting on the Head Lessons

Synopsis:
We open the show this time is another TV spoof, this time of UK show *The Money Programme*. The sketch itself is fairly lightweight, essentially consisting of Idle waxing lyrical about money and then leaping onto the desk to deliver a song in praise of it. It makes for an intro to the credits, anyhow, and thence into the rather contentious 'Fraud Film Director' sketch. It is contentious because the basis of the sketch would never be accepctible today. The general theme is an Elizabethan court scene directed by a Japanese film director, which is called 'Erizabeth L' and has all of the letters L and R mixed up. The director is found to be impersonating an Italian director, but not before the terms 'nip' and 'slit-eyes' have been used. Much like the previous episode, this is still happily shown, and the probable reason is that *Python* is so absurdist that to claim offence at something which was in keeping with the time would seem as odd as the differing standards. The other notable thing about this Elizabethan scene is that almost everybody is riding motorised bicycles, for no apparent reason. It isn't the team's finest work, to be honest.

A weak start then, but things soon pick up. After an inspired Gilliam animation of a man being told 'Hands Up!' and complying by raising around a dozen arms, we are into another of those working-class homes so beloved of the team. In this case, the bizarre dinner items being served up, including 'Unjugged rabbit fish' and 'Strawberry tart with three rats', are the first point of interest, but this soon changes with the discovery of a dead bishop in the next room. The 'church police', led by Palin, swoop in and make the arrest. We are then, via another animation, into a party of jungle explorers (including Carol Cleveland in a moustache), who arrive at a clearing where this part of the untamed jungle has been transformed into a sophisticated al fresco restaurant. The waiter (Palin in absurd blackface make up) greets the party but, while attempting to take their order, has to leap into action and rush into the undergrowth when two customers are killed, by a gorilla and a poison dart respectively. As they finish ordering, jungle drums are heard and we cut away to a BBC announcer (Idle) informing us that, owing to the extreme violence, and also nudity, in the next scene, we will be shown a clip from 'Ken Russell's Gardening Club 1958' instead. This consists of a nude woman and a city gent running into a flower bed, followed swiftly by two nuns, two Vikings, a gumby and a large pantomime goose.

We return to the action with the party being led as prisoners through the jungle. Things then become ever more anarchic, with various people having to find the place in the script, film of a London-based hero hearing of the plight from a hopeless actor and a 'breaking the fourth wall' scene where they realise they are not alone if someone is filming them ... and someone else filming them

74

in turn. Inspector Baboon of The Yard appears in order to arrest another fraud director, and the credits roll. All is not finished, however, as the 'BBC Globe' comes up with a voice announcing 'another six minutes of *Monty Python*'. At this point, we are now in the classic 'Argument Sketch'.

In case there is anyone still unfamiliar with this *Python* Great, the sketch sees a man (Palin) turning up at the 'Argument Clinic', and paying for a five-minute argument. First going by mistake to the 'abuse' room, he finds Cleese and enjoys a short argument about what constitutes an argument. Cleese then terminates things by ringing his bell, signalling the end suspiciously early. He refuses to argue again until he is paid, which he is, and they continue by arguing about whether he has been paid or not. It's marvellously timed stuff, by both of the protagonists. The sketch concludes by Palin going to complain, again entering the wrong room and receiving lessons in being hit over the head. Much head-hitting with a large wooden mallet ensues before Inspector Flying Fox Of The Yard enters to arrest them under Section 21 of the Strange Sketch Act.

Comments.
The secretary in the 'Argument Clinic' is played, once again, by Rita Davis. The Fred Tomlinson Singers are once more on hand, this time to accompany 'The Money Song', which is written by Eric Idle and John Gould. Everyone else in this episode is uncredited. The Welsh Harp in the opening sketch is played by Sheila Bromberg.

The three locations glimpsed by the fearless jungle explorers in the distance are: The sacred volcano Andu, which no man has seen before; The London Brick Company; The forbidden plateau of Roiurama, the Lost World.

Author's Pick.
There isn't really any competition here. It's a rather middling quality episode all told, but it contains 'The Argument Sketch'. Nothing is going to beat that.

Episode Four: Blood, Devastation, Death, War and Horror
First aired 9 November 1972
Sketches include:
The Man Who Speaks in Anagrams
Merchant Banker
Killer Houses
Mary Recruitment Office
The Man Who Makes People Laugh Uncontrollably
Gestures in a Televised Talk
The Pantomime Horse is a Secret Agent

Synopsis:
This superb episode begins with stock footage of disasters and horror, cutting

to Palin presenting a programme entitled 'Blood, Devastation, Death, War and Horror', which turns out to be a chat show promising a man who does gardening. First up, though, we have Idle as the opening guest, portraying a man who speaks in anagrams. A typical Idle sketch, full of clever and involved wordplay, the list of Shakespeare plays among other things butchered by the anagram form is brought to an end by his storming off after accusations of having used a Spoonerism. The credits follow before Cleese appears as the masterfully odious merchant banker struggling to grasp the whole concept of charity when faced with Jones as the meek fellow collecting for the orphans. In the end, the hapless Jones disappears through a trapdoor and things reach new levels of surreality as two pantomime horses enter and are told the bank can only afford to keep one on, so they must fight to the death. This spills over to a voice-over, again by Cleese, describing with the aid of film 'life and death struggles' between sea lions, limpets, an ant and a wolf, some nature documentary makers, the pantomime horses again (one is hit by the 16-stone weight) before finally giving us a pantomime goose versus Sir Terence Rattigan and a pantomime Princess Margaret and a breakfast tray.

An excellent animated sequence has the announcer from the previous sketch meeting a sudden demise, followed by the cautionary tale of the 'Killer Houses'. This leads us to the anagram theme continued by an Army Recruitment Office, misspelt as Mary. Idle enters seeing an offer for work in a sketch, and he asks the recruiting Chapman about any more effeminate regiments, particularly those working in fabric and interior design. Chapman directs him without hesitation to the Durham Light Infantry. After a while Idle complains that his lines don't get any laughs, so they reappear on the top deck of a bus where, yet again Conductor Chapman steals all the laughs. An interjection showing Jones as a completely unremarkable city gent sending anyone he speaks to into uncontrollable hilarity follows before the previous sketch is wrapped up by the complaining Idle taking a barrage of slapstick gags from the clown-costumed Chapman.

We then move to Dutch TV for Mr Orbital-5 (Palin) becoming increasingly bogged down in the question of whether viewers will be able to differentiate between a pause and ceasing to speak. To this end, he develops and demonstrates a series of such gestures to clarify. The BBC globe interrupts this with a break to provide work for a depressed announcer (Cleese) who has not been able to announce since his wife ('Joe-jums') has been struggling with post-natal depression. Encouraged by wife and friend, he struggles through, and the only part of Palin's epic monologue we hear is 'paste down the edge of the sailor's uniform, until the word 'Maudling' is almost totally obscured' – another roasting for popular target Reginald Maudling. This is followed by Richard Baker reading the news, which we cannot hear due to Cleese being congratulated on getting through his announcement, but the sight of him replicating Palin's hand gestures is hilarious. We get to hear the last few words of his report, which are of course 'until the word 'Maudling' is almost totally obscured'. Finally, there is the glorious location film 'The Pantomime Horse is a Secret Agent', which has a British panto horse chasing a fiendish Russian one, including a truly bizarre scene in which they both ride actual horses. The end credits are, of course, all in anagram form.

Comments.
According to Michael Palin, during the climactic Pantomime Horse chase, he was actually driving the car while wearing the horse outfit and he could hardly see where he was going through the mask.

Richard Baker, who appears as himself in this episode, was a BBC Television newsreader for almost 30 years and was the first man to read the news on BBC TV in 1954. He also narrated and presented a range of other programmes until 2007, and died in 2018 aged 93. The images behind his news broadcast in this episode include Richard Nixon, Lord Snowdon, the White House, Princess Margaret, the Houses of Parliament, a pair of naked breasts, a scrubbing brush, a man with a stoat through his head, Margaret Thatcher, a toilet, a Scotsman lying on his back, a corkscrew, then-Prime Minister Edward Heath and a pair of false teeth in a glass.

In the opening credits sequence, the show's name is in anagram form as 'Tony M. Nyphot's Flying Risccu'.

The music played during the Panto Horse Chase is 'Devil's Gallop', the theme music to *Dick Barton Special Agent*. The music behind the interviewer's introduction during the opening sketch is called 'Newsroom', composed by Simon Campbell.

The images of death and horror in the opening scene are as follows: trains crashing (silent movie footage), car crash (gangster film footage), train falling from bridge (silent film special effects footage), an erupting volcano, a burning, sinking ship (this is the 'Torrey Canyon') and forest fire footage.

Author's Pick.
Another masterful episode with many high points. The climactic Panto horse chase is hilarious, while Cleese's banker is masterfully portrayed, to name but two. However, the whole 'Gestures in a televised talk' section, culminating in Richard Baker's priceless contribution is the one which gets top billing from me this time out.

Episode Five: The All-England Summarise Proust Competition

First aired 16 November 1972
Sketches include:
Summarise Proust Competition
Hairdressers Climb Up Mount Everest
Fire Brigade

Party Hints with Veronica Smalls
Language Laboratory
Travel Agent
Anne Elk's Theory on Brontosauruses

Synopsis:

Unusually, this episode actually begins with the opening credits! Following this departure, we are straight into the 'All England Summarise Proust Competition', in which contestants have fifteen seconds to summarise the seven volumes of the great French author's *A La Recherché du Temps Perdu*. The first contestant, Harry Bagot from Luton (Chapman), makes an excellent fist of putting the whole work into context, but after doing that he only reaches Page One of the first volume, *Swann's Way*. Before leaving the stage he lists his hobbies as 'strangling animals, golf and masturbating'. Next up is a hopelessly nervous Ronald Rutherford of Leicester (Palin), who keeps forgetting the names of the characters and locations. Finally come the Bolton Choral Society, who take the entire time singing in perfect contrapuntal madrigal form 'Proust in his first book wrote about, wrote about...'. All three fail dismally, so the compère Arthur Mee elects to award the prize to 'the girl with the biggest tits'. As the 'show' ends, the *Python* end credits roll – the opening credits may have run at the beginning, but the end credits have followed within five minutes.

After this, we see an account of an attempt on Everest by a group of hairdressers after the sketch is forced to restart accompanied by a bizarre and hideous clown waving from the side of the screen. Most of the sketch is standard early '70s 'camp hairdresser' material until it is revealed that fourteen different expeditions are attempting the climb simultaneously, including a team of French chiropodists and a Glasgow male voice choir. The hairdressers elect to open a salon. From this we move to a little old lady (Jones) calling the Fire Brigade, who we see busying themselves with hobbies and discussing cookery, and taking the phone off the hook so they won't be disturbed. Her son Mervyn (Cleese) enters and advises her to go and play the cello, as it turns out their hamster is unwell, and this may save him. He, in turn, tries to get the fire brigade, but the operator bogs him down in asking about his shoes. This begins a running gag whereby characters on the phone stop, remove their shoes and tell the person on the other end their size. The hamster sadly dies, only to be covered up by the 'Charlie George Football Annual'. At this point, the door opens and a large African warrior (a blacked-up Chapman) complete with spear, shield and suitcases, announces 'Hello mummy!', and we learn this is her other son Eamonn, who has been in Dublin and is eager to talk about the possibility of a constitutional settlement. The fire brigade eventually makes an appointment to come the following Friday, but they climb in through the window only to settle down and enjoy a party.

On the subject of parties, we are taken to 'Party Hints with Veronica Smalls', in which Idle as Smalls takes us through how best to deal with a communist uprising during a party. This leads to a rather odd sketch set in a 'Language laboratory', in which Cleese is being shown round a room in which people at cubicles are earnestly practising different accents, including a rather controversial South African one (even for the time) which consists largely of Idle reciting the words 'Kill the blecks. Kill the blecks. Rhodesia. Smith'. Eventually, we discover Cleese wants to learn a routine to make himself popular, and while the 'Life and soul of the party tape' is searched for, the men in the cubicles break into a peculiar 1930s song routine.

From here it's into a Travel Agent's, where Idle enters to talk to Mr Bounder (Palin) about an 'adventure holiday' to India. Idle introduces himself as 'Mr Smoketoomuch', and when Palin makes the obvious joke of 'you'd better cut down then' he is astonished because this has never occurred to him. After explaining that he cannot say the letter C, and being advised to cure this by pretending instances of C are in fact K, he explains that he saw their details in the 'bolour supplement', and that he is tired of package holidays, and embarks on a long and rambling rant about holidaymakers abroad. While this is boring Palin to distraction, his secretary (Cleveland) beckons us down a hallway to a studio in which Chapman is interviewing a woman named 'Anne Elk' (Cleese in hilarious drag) who has a new theory about Brontosauruses. After an interminable time coaxing her to actually explain her theory, it turns out to consist of 'they are thin at one end, go thick in the middle and then thin again at the other end'. She starts to explain that she has another theory, but we head back to the Travel Agent, and things are broken up amid machine gun fire.

Comments.
This episode fell foul of the BBC censors in two places when originally broadcast. The line about 'strangling animals, golf and masturbating' in the 'Summarise Proust Competition' was cut absurdly to be 'strangling animals, golf'(pause) – followed by an inexplicable audience laugh. Thankfully this was later restored. Similarly, in the Travel Agent, Mr Smoketoomuch (who cannot pronounce the letter C) had the line 'What a silly bunt' immediately removed!

The Fred Tomlinson Singers are on duty again in this episode, playing the Bolton Choral Society and the Fire Brigade.

The judges (all cardboard cut-outs) in the 'Summarise Proust Competition' are as follows: Arthur and Eric Bedser (twin brothers who played Cricket for Surrey in the 1940s and 1950s – England international Alec was far more successful); Stuart Surridge (another cricketer, who captained Surrey in the 1950s, and came from a famous cricket-bat making family); Omar Sharif (Egyptian actor); Laurie Fishlock (a rather unheralded cricketer from the 1930s and 1940s – yes, he played for Surrey); Peter May (cricketer, and yes, Surrey) and Yehudi Menuhin (virtuoso violinist and not, despite claims in this episode, the President of Surrey County Cricket Club. However, two decades later, he was, in fact, made a life peer, as Baron Menuhin, of Stoke d'Abernon in the

County of Surrey!). This obsession with post-war Surrey is likely to have come from Jones, who lived in the county for fifteen years growing up.

The Proust work *A La Recherché du Temps Perdu* was originally known in English as *Remembrance of Things Past*, the title used when it was first translated. However, a 1992 translation used the slightly more literal *In Search Of Lost Time*, and this has become the generally accepted English title. There are those, however, who still believe the earlier title to be a more poetic and evocative one.

Cleese's Anne Elk character is generally accepted to have been inspired by Chapman's partner David Sherlock, who would often talk in a similarly roundabout fashion.

Author's Pick.
Not the greatest episode overall, with once again some good ideas not being best realised. The Proust competition is the best-remembered, and Chapman's delightfully absurd Africa warrior home from Dublin is another highlight, but the short but brilliant Cleese performance as Anne Elk just shades it for me.

Episode Six: The War Against Pornography
First aired 23 November 1972
Sketches include:
Tory Housewives Clean-up Campaign
Gumby Brain Specialist
Molluscs
Report on the Minister reports
Tuesday Documentary
Children's Story
Expedition to Lake Pahoe
The Silliest Interview We've Ever Had
The Silliest Sketch We've Ever Done

Synopsis:
The episode, this time out, opens with a photo of Conservative Prime Minister of the time Edward Heath, accompanied by some jingoistic narration shows a gang of 'pepperpot' tory women mobilising themselves to break strikes by beating up the militants, chase lazy workers back into factories etc. We also see them taking their revenge on the permissive society, as an art gallery is invaded and clothes added to all of the nudes. Speaking of which, the nude Terry Jones at the organ predictably ends the sketch and ushers in the credits.

Following this, we see Palin as a gumby entering a doctor's office. After crying 'Doctor!' repeatedly, and demolishing the desk, gumby doctor Cleese enters. It appears Gumby Palin requires brain surgery (the much-repeated phrase 'my brain hurts' is born here), and we cut to an operating theatre with *Doctor Kildare* music. Surgeon Chapman is quite level headed and clear thinking, until he calls for 'moustache' and 'handkerchief', and morphs into a gumby. The patient speaks, and they realise they have forgotten the anaesthetic, which arrives through the wall and is administered by hitting him on the lead with the gas cylinder.

We head next to a sitting room where a couple are watching live badminton coverage and duly smash the TV. They are inexplicably wearing ballroom dancing attire, complete with numbers. A ring on the doorbell sees Cleese as Mr Zorba, arriving to present a documentary on molluscs, which he does by walking in behind a board with a TV screen shaped hole in it and talking to them from behind it. Bored, they attempt to switch him off, but he gets away with it by concentrating on the licentious sex lives of these various mollusc species, and they go from bored to disgusted fascination. They thank him for an interesting programme, and we cut to newsreader Palin as he talks about Parliament, with references to such positions as The Minister For Not Listening To People. This abruptly changes in tone repeatedly, accompanied by captions, to classic serial, documentary, children's story and party political broadcast, ending as *Match Of The Day*, complete with celebrating footballers in slow-motion romantic embraces.

After an apology to politicians which manages to abuse them still further, we are off to a Royal Naval expedition to Lake Pahoe, which, oddly, is located at 22a Runcorn Avenue, just off Blenheim Crescent. The man imparting this knowledge is the party leader Sir Jane Russell, interviewed by Cleese along with naval colleague Dorothy Lamour (another man). As Cleese talks to them, he gradually changes shot by shot into Long John Silver and is replaced by a second interviewer after a short psychedelic animated advert for the Royal Navy. Sir John Cunningham is now the spokesman, apologising for his colleagues, and also apologising for the small amount of cannibalism still present in the service, underlined by one of the sailors gnawing on a human leg. The party visit 22 Runcorn Avenue and are directed to 22a, which is the basement, in which a couple sit submerged in water with breathing apparatus, complaining about the damp and the sharks. They refuse to let them in and the expedition has failed.

To wrap things up, we go to Cleese as another TV presenter, interviewing Mr Badger (Chapman), a Scottish historical expert who theorises that the Magna Carta was, in fact, a piece of chewing gum. He explains this, but will only do so via mime, and concludes by putting his finger up his nose. Cleese announces that he is the silliest person he has ever interviewed but asks him out to dinner anyway. We cut to the restaurant where Badger explains that his wife left him during a goalless draw between Aberdeen and Raith Rovers, and orders whisky for starter, main course and dessert, but demands a bottle of wine to accompany it. Together with disgruntled waiter Palin, they all agree the sketch is far too silly, and they get up and abandon it.

Comments.

The underwater scene in the basement was filmed in a swimming pool at Butlin's Holiday Camp in Bognor, after which the *Python* team were reprimanded in writing for their refusal to follow health and safety procedures regarding scuba gear – which, considering the lack of any such protocol in those days, would suggest a rather reckless approach to the filming indeed!

The various government departments in the political speech are as follows: the Minister for not listening to people; the Shadow Minister for judging people at first sight to be marginally worse than they actually are; the Minister for inserting himself in between chairs and walls in men's clubs; the Minister for running upstairs two at a time, flinging the door open and saying 'Ha, ha! Caught you, Mildred'; the Under-Secretary for making deep growling noises; the ex-Minister for delving deep into a black satin bag and producing a tube of Euthymol toothpaste; the Junior Minister for being frightened by any kind of farm machinery; the Under-Secretary of State for hiding from Terence Rattigan; the Department of stealing packets of bandages from the self-service counter at Timothy Whites and selling them again at a considerable profit.

Euthymol toothpaste, as referred to above, was a brand of antiseptic, fluoride-free toothpaste which was bright pink and had a strong medicinal taste. Amazingly, it proved popular. It still exists today but with a new formulation. Timothy Whites, also listed above, were a British chain of dispensing chemists who eventually disappeared in 1985. Terrence Rattigan was, of course, a British dramatist, perhaps most famous for *The Winslow Boy*. He died in 1977.

While the 'tory women' are demonstrating outside BBC Television Centre to clean up television programming, they hold aloft a sign 'Wanted Dead Or Alive' alongside a photo of Robert Robinson. Robinson was a rather clean-cut broadcaster known for family programmes, but he was the unfortunate interviewer in 1965 on the satirical show *BBC3* when Kenneth Tynan became the first man to say the word 'fuck' on British television (though there have since been claims that three other people had done so already, although not in Tynan's calculated manner). The women also wear armbands reading 'PP'. This is short for 'PepperPots', the nickname for these 'old lady' characters.

Author's Pick.

This is another somewhat patchy episode, with good ideas not being as well-executed as they might be to do them full justice. The clear winner here has to be the 'Gumby Brain Surgery'. 'My brain hurts!!'

Episode Seven: Salad Days

First aired 30 November 1972
Sketches include:
Biggles Dictates a Letter
Climbing the North Face of the Uxbridge Road

Lifeboat
Storage Jars
TV is Bad For Your Eyes
The Show so Far
Cheese Shop sketch
Philip Jenkinson / Salad Days
The News with Richard Baker

Synopsis:
At the beginning of this episode, we see Jones' usual organist figure walking to his instrument fully clothed for once, though order is restored as, after a single note, his clothes are hoisted to the ceiling, and the other Pythons appear as a naked quartet. After the opening credits, we see fictional RAF hero Biggles in the unusual act of dictating a letter to his secretary. Amid the predictable misunderstandings around when he is dictating and when he is merely talking (he dons a pair of antlers to differentiate between the two), we see him arguing with his secretary that he is not Spanish and shooting his faithful sidekick Algy when he discovers he is gay (that era-dating material again). The pantomime Princess Margaret makes another appearance, lumbering out of the cupboard. There is also the first of several interjections from random people asking the question 'lemon curry?' for no discernible reason, as a running gag.

An animated sequence prevents the sketch from outstaying its welcome too much before cutting to a mountaineering expedition, attempting to climb the north face of the Uxbridge Road. Struggling along the pavements with ropes, pitons and full mountaineering gear is a delightfully surreal *Python* idea, but can't last too long and still sustain the joke. It doesn't and passes in perfect time to Palin's lifeboatman crashing in through the door of a kitchen (where Jones portrays a lady stuffing a chicken with what appears to be a cat) from a howling gale and spray behind him. When she insists it is not a lifeboat but 24 Parker Street, he goes back out of the door and sees a regular back garden. Several of his colleagues enter in similar fashion, and Jones goes out to get them cakes. Unsurprisingly going out of the front door does, in fact, take her out onto a lifeboat deck in a howling gale, and she struggles to a hatch from where Mrs Edwards (Chapman) is serving morning coffee and afternoon tea to passing ships. This idea overstays its welcome before we cut to a TV programme about storage jars, called appropriately enough 'Storage Jars'. It cuts to Jones as a reporter under fire in war-torn Bolivia, who braves the shells and bullets to report on a display of local jars, before a classic Gilliam animation of a device repeatedly emerging from a TV set to torture the viewer's eyeballs ends with the expected pay-off of 'Turn that TV off dear, it's bad for your eyes'.

After Jones recaps the show so far in dry, dull tones and is hit on the head with a large hammer, we are into the celebrated 'Cheese Shop' sketch, with Cleese as the customer in Palin's cheese emporium who discovers bit by bit that it has no cheese. There is also a surreal accompaniment of Jones and Chapman as businessmen dancing to bouzouki music in the background. Clearly attempting to emulate the Parrot Sketch, it cannot be said to succeed although Cleese's frustrated yet despairingly patient customer is played to perfection.

The final segment has Idle as film critic Philip Jenkinson earnestly discussing the genre of 'Cheese Westerns' before introducing a clip of a remake of the musical *Salad Days* by director Sam Peckinpah (known for such violent works as *Straw Dogs*). This gloriously violent scene has a group of straw-boatered 'bright young things' from the 1920s, gleefully talking about playing tennis until a stray tennis ball to the eye begins a cycle of violent accidents including impalement by tennis racquets and a keyboard, and pianist Cleese getting his hands chopped off by the piano lid falling on them. Jenkinson himself is gunned down while praising the film, and a profuse apology for the bad taste of the sketch on behalf of the entire team follows after the end credits roll.

The final ending to the episode has Richard Baker again reading the news, referencing Storage Jars in particular, and ending with the question 'lemon curry?' before an 'interlude' of waves on a beach uses up time as Cleese, as a historical figure, explains that it is using up time.

Comments.

Filming of the Lifeboat scenes took place in Folkestone Harbour and had to be halted several times as Cleese was being violently seasick. Driving back to town later with Chapman, he began to feel a little better and was advised by the medically trained Chapman that he should eat something. He suggested some cheese, but they could only find a chemist's shop open at the time. They joked about them needing medicinal cheese, and that Chapman could write a prescription for it, and the idea for 'Cheese Shop' was born. They tried to write about a chemist selling medicinal cheese on prescription, but it turned into the final version of the sketch. All of the cheeses listed are genuine, with the exception of Venezuelan Beaver Cheese, which was invented by Cleese. He has commented that, in those pre-internet days, he had to research the sketch by standing in a delicatessen slavishly writing down the name of every cheese on display in a large cabinet, to suspicious stares from the staff. The bouzouki in the shop has been variously credited as being played by session musicians Joe Moretti or Alan Parker. The song is entitled 'Grecian Nights'.

Filming of the climbing of the Uxbridge Road actually took place on South Ealing Road, also in West London.

Philip Jenkinson was a prolific film critic and BBC TV presenter, hosting the programme *Film Night* for several years. During the 1970s he was well known to viewers for his weekly column in the listings magazine *Radio Times*, reviewing the week's films.

The material regarding Biggles' gay partners Algy and Ginger appears to have two points. Firstly, it is undoubtedly satirising the close relationship between male fictional characters of the pre-1960s, and indeed speculation which had been made by readers about the *Biggles* series of books in particular. However, given that Biggles himself is portrayed by Chapman, who was by this time openly gay himself, makes it very likely that this was a comment on the rising amount of violence towards gay men as the 'gay rights' movement grew. The *Python* team were all supporters of Chapman's lifestyle, and such incidents as the previous episode's killing of the 'homosexual whelks' by jumping on them likely grew from the same inspiration. It is this kind of progressive thinking that *Python* was known for which contributes to many sketches still being shown uncut, despite sitting uneasily with contemporary values.

There seems to be a continuity error during the 'Biggles' sketch unless it is deliberate. Chapman announces, and demonstrates, that he will wear a pair of anthers when he is dictating and take them off when he is not. As the sketch progresses, however, he slips into a pattern of taking them off when he is dictating and putting them on when he is not, as the complete opposite.

The secretary in the 'Biggles' sketch, Miss Bladder, is played by Nicki Howarth. A 1970s actress, her screen roles were nevertheless very limited, with her only non-*Python* credits being a 1971 film called *Not Tonight Darling* and an episode of *The Generation Game*, though she did also appear uncredited in an episode of *Are You Being Served*.

At the end of the animated 'TV Is Bad For Your Eyes' segment, the fairy godfather from 'programme control' once again used the face of Paul Fox, with whom the Pythons had crossed swords before.

Author's Pick.
The most well-known sketch on offer here is, without doubt, 'Cheese Shop', but it must be said that despite the sublime performances from Palin and Cleese, it is a little too derivative of the Parrot Sketch, and its single joke is hard to sustain. In the absence of any truly standout sketched in this episode, I am going to go with the animated 'TV Is Bad For Your Eyes' as the highlight.

Episode Eight: The Cycling Tour
First aired 7 December 1972
No sketches as such

Synopsis:
A radical departure for *Python*, this self-contained half-hour story is their first foray into a relatively linear, if bizarre, narrative. Even the normal opening credits and theme tune are dispensed with as a simple caption of 'The Cycling Tour' accompanies the appearance of Palin's bobble-hatted Reg Pither, embarking on a cycling tour of North Cornwall. Mostly written by Palin and Jones, they each take one single main role apiece while the other Pythons take smaller parts throughout.

Unsurprisingly, the episode opens with Pither falling off his bike, and indeed doing so several times, as he proceeds to bore assorted locals with his inane wittering about sandwiches and damage to his packed lunch. After one such tumble, he decides that, as he is getting the pump caught in his trousers, shorts and a shorter pump should be the answer. He asks a local woman whether there is a bicycle repair shop in the village, to which she replies 'There's only one shop here', and points to a large sign reading 'BICYCLE PUMP CENTRE. SPECIALISTS IN SHORTER BICYCLE PUMPS', and another announcing 'SHORT PUMPS AVAILABLE HERE'. 'What a stroke of luck', he muses. Unfortunately, he again falls off after getting the pump caught in his sock.

We head next for a doctor's surgery, where Pither has gone to ask directions from the clearly irritated GP (Idle), who nevertheless gives him a prescription for directions which he takes to a chemist. In a pub, he sits next to Cleese and Cleveland, a married man with a young mistress, who are having a crisis around him leaving his wife of sixteen years. Pither gloriously ruins this by confusing the distressed Cleese with enquiries about the availability of Tizer in the area, and their tryst is destroyed forever. The next crash sees Pither united with Jones as Mr Gulliver, who rescues him in his car where they talk animatedly about the damage to his various snacks. Gulliver, it turns out, is obsessed with snack food safety and is working on such things as indestructible cheese sandwiches and a tomato which can sense danger and escape. A tomato immediately leaps out of the car, and they crash again, causing Gulliver to lose his memory and believe he is singer Clodagh Rogers.

At this point, via an accident-prone hospital Casualty Department, they turn up in southern France, as Gulliver begins to change personality again into Trotsky, disappointing two autograph hunters and French Clodagh fans who delight in singing her hit 'Jack In A Box'. Soon after, they arrive in Russia and book into a Young Men's Anti-Christian Association hostel, while Pither heads for the British Embassy. Here he meets Chapman as 'Mr Atkinson', an obviously Oriental man dressed head to toe in flowing traditional Chinese garb and speaking with a manic Chinese accent. Escaping from there, amid a peasant's Bingo revolt, he is invited by three obviously shady men, who deny they are secret police, to a 'clambake', and he accompanies them to a Communist party meeting in Moscow called the 42nd International Clambake, where Gulliver/ Trotsky is due to speak. Unfortunately, at this point he changes again into believing he is Eartha Kitt, singing 'I'm just an old fashioned girl' to such success that he gets booked for another show. Pither is not so lucky and gets sentenced to death by firing squad.

Fortunately for him, the firing squad, commanded by Cleese, are so incompetent they all miss. Twice. Claiming that 'he moved'. Meanwhile Gulliver regains his mind after changing into Edward Heath on stage and getting hit by a dangerous vegetable thrown at the stage. He runs to Pither, climbs the wall to join him as the firing squad charge with bayonets, but a caption announces their miraculous escape. Their warm farewell sees the end credits roll, but there is one more surprise. Throughout the Cornwall scenes we have seen glimpses of two animated monsters peeping over the trees. Just as we think Gilliam has done hardly any animation this time, they check the coast is now clear, leap into the open and begin a spirited rendition of 'Jack In A Box'. An inspired ending to a tremendous, and highly original, episode.

Comments.

After this episode aired, Palin received a tin of Devon cream addressed to Mr Pither via the BBC, On picking it up, he found a letter with it from a dairy owner from Bovey Tracey (location of the first crash), thanking him for the free publicity, correcting the pronunciation from Bovey to Burvey, and finishing up with 'I think you are all mad'.

At an event organised by Charisma Records in 1975 at the Marquee Club, London, Palin met Jimmy Page and Robert Plant from Led Zeppelin, and was delighted to discover that not only were they *Python* fans but also that they were particularly fond of this very episode.

One of the autograph hunters in France is played, uncredited, by Chapman's adopted son John Tomiczek.

In Pither's cell is a poster announcing the upcoming concert with Eartha Kitt headlining over 'Burgess and MacLean' (famous as Russian spies from the 1960s, alongside Kim Philby), ' Marshall Bulganin and Charlie' (Nikolai Bulganin, Minister of Defence under Kruschev) and 'Peter Cook and Dudley Moore'. As Gulliver escapes, another poster announces 'Next Week: Clodagh Rogers'.

There is a moment after Gulliver becomes Trotsky where we see old footage of Lenin apparently singing 'If I Ruled The World'. This was originally to be followed by a Gilliam animation of 'Lenin Chartbusters Volume III', but this was sadly cut.

Idle appears as a military man several times in this episode, pointing out the current locations on a map. There is an error as he announces at one point that Monte Carlo is '500 miles west of Bilbao', rather than east as the script dictates. 500 miles west of Bilbao would be in the Atlantic ocean.

Clodagh Rogers was a successful performer throughout the 1960s and 1970s, but her most well-known song remains her 1971 Eurovision Song Contest entry 'Jack In A Box'. The music to which Mr Pither cycles is the waltz from Act Two of *Faust* by Gounod.

Author's Pick.

There is no sketch to pick out from this episode, simply because there are strictly speaking no individual sketches. There are however several scenes which stand out even in this excellent episode: the Russian soldier rushing to the firing squad with a note which turns out to read 'Carry on with the execution' is a particularly glorious subverting of convention, while Chapman's over-the-top Chinese 'Mr Atkinson' is a masterpiece of broad comedy.

Episode Nine: The Nude Organist
First aired 14 December 1972
Sketches include:
Bomb on Plane
A Naked Man
Construction Projects
Mortuary Hour
The Olympic Hide-and-seek Final
The Cheap-Laughs
Bull-fighting
Prices on the Planet Algon

Synopsis:
We are back to familiar ground again in terms of abandoning any hope of
a linear narrative thread. We open onboard a plane, with Idle's irritating
Scotsman Mr Badger entering the cabin with the news that there is a bomb
on board and he will reveal the location for a thousand pounds. He is quickly
bargained down to a pound, at which point he first forgets where it is, then
gives away the location. A clipboard-wielding director bemoans the ruination of
the sketch, and we cut to Jones as the naked organist in a field surrounded by
hangers-on. Wearing a fine silk robe with the name Noel Coward crossed out,
he is talking earnestly about his significance in the show before they realise
they are on camera, take the robe off him, and we begin.

After the title sequence, we head to a construction site in Bristol where a
voice-over informs us that this is the first housing project being built entirely
by characters from 19th Century English literature, several of whom we
meet. Then it is over to what an announcer informs us is an eighteen-level
M1 Motorway Interchange, the first of its kind to be constructed entirely
by characters from Milton's *Paradise Lost*. A foreman (Jones) explains the
problems they have encountered with the angels, demons and serpents not
getting along, and that he has had to split the forces of good and evil into
separate shift patterns.

We are not yet done with the construction projects, however, as we meet El
Mystico and Janet (the latter last-seen as assistant to another magician, Kargol,
in Series One) who are building blocks of flats by hypnosis. This is incredibly
fast and cost-effective, with the only drawback being that if the tenants stop
believing in the buildings, they will immediately fall down. We are then taken
through a potted biography of Janet, who appears rather over-qualified for the
role of Glamorous Assistant, holding several world championships and a Nobel
prize. We also learn that she has become ever more fastidious in the matter
of turning people in to the police for trivial offences, for which most of them
are hanged, as it becomes clear that the repeal of the death penalty is rather
often simply being forgotten about – a fact which the authorities are at pains to
deflect attention from. We go to a mortuary which is extremely busy owing to

the regular executions, but where the employees still find time to listen to the radio programme 'Mortuary Hour with Shirley Bassey'.

While these sketches are going on, a running joke occurs of Idle's irritating Scotsman offering not to interrupt them for a pound. After another of these interruptions, and a surreal self-referencing animation which has Gilliam showing us how to do animation, culminating in flying saucers changing into World War One helmets and thence to soldiers in a trench, we head to London for the final of the Olympic Hide And Seek event, in which the Paraguayan competitor (Jones) has to find the British hider (Chapman) in less than 11 years, 2 months, 26 days, 9 hours, 3 minutes, 27.4 seconds, after which time, in the first leg, the Paraguayan was found in a sweet shop in Kilmarnock. Chapman heads at pace to Sardinia, where he hides in a castle, occasionally peeping around the corner. Eventually he is found dramatically, eleven years later, in a dead heat time, and the replay is scheduled for the next day.

From there it is on to a respectable suburban couple, Cleese and Cleveland, who are entertaining their neighbours, the Cheap-Laughs, portrayed by Jones in an absurd clown outfit and his wife Chapman. After an insufferable evening of slapstick they are left alone and we learn that they are tired of having to try to keep up with the Cheap-Laughs. They discuss this in bed, which folds up into a wall to reveal the studio of the 'Probe' show, which is investigating bullfighting, which we are told, is being very unfair on the poor Spaniard who has no horns or hooves.

This is a short bridge to the final sketch, concerning the discovery of the planet Algon in the Aldebaran system, and in particular a lengthy discussion about the exorbitant prices of shopping there, and the availability of erotic lingerie. When this sketch ends, after the cameras 'strike crumpet' in the shape of an attractive woman running between the rocks, we return to the Scotsman who has accepted the job of reading the credits for the sum of 40p, which he does. They are not displayed, and we learn that the show was produced by Ian McNaughton 'for 92p and a bottle of Bell's Whisky'. The 16-ton weight falls on him.

Comments.

Most of the female parts this week are Carol Cleveland, but Lyn Ashley (as 'Mrs Idle') plays the girl on Algon, while a reporter interviewing announcer Cleese before the credits is portrayed by Marie Anderson, in her only credited TV role.

The 'Paradise Lost' scene was filmed at a construction site on the A40 at Denham, west of London. Work was actually going on during filming and Palin writes in his diaries that they would try to time the shots for when the biggest bulldozers came into view, so they would be waiting around only to spring into fast action to attempt to time their filming correctly.

After the Hide And Seek event, the following sketch is introduced as being in a sitting room with the words 'Sorry it's just a sitting room, but the bank account's a bit low after the appallingly expensive production of 'Clochemerle...'. This is referencing a BBC nine-episode comedy series of that name which had recently been produced, about the intrigue and politics surrounding plans to install a public urinal in a French village. Starring Peter Ustinov and Roy Dotrice, it has since sunk almost without trace, and I have never seen it, but those who have tend to claim that it was excellent.

Author's Pick.
There are several entertaining sketches in this fairly strong episode, but I am in no doubt as to nominate the marvellously unhinged 'Olympic Hide And Seek Final'. Good all-round, however.

Episode Ten: E. Henry Thripshaw's Disease
First aired 21 December 1972
Sketches include:
Tudor Jobs Agency
Silly Disturbances
The Free Repetition of Doubtful Words Sketch
'Is There?'... Life after Death?
The Man Who Says Words in the Wrong Order
Thripshaw's Disease
Sherry-drinking Vicar

Synopsis:
The episode begins as we see Chapman entering a building with a sign reading 'Tudor Jobs Agency'. Once inside, we see Jones in Tudor garb behind the counter, and we realise that this is - quite literally - a Tudor job agency, in that it only provides Tudor jobs, such as accompanying Walter Raleigh or building the Globe Theatre. After a sob story about not placing anyone in a job since 1625, Chapman then asks about dirty books, and the true nature of this pornographic bookshop becomes clear. With a coded request about raising the drawbridge, a wall slides open, and he enters a small bookshop populated by salesman Idle and several seedy customers, including Gilliam who arrives at the counter with £540 worth of magazines but decides to have the top one only. The door slides open a second time at the passphrase, and a policeman, Superintendent Gaskell, enters in full Tudor garb. Everyone immediately addresses him as Sir Philip Sydney, but he insists it is a disguise while calling for Sgt Gaskell, who isn't with him. When the customers, and then Idle, leave through the side door, he follows, only to materialise in a garden in the time of Elizabeth The First. Everyone greets him as Sir Philip Sydney, of course.

For a while, he enjoys the reputation Sir Philip clearly has but is soon summoned away to where the Spanish are landing. He rushes down to the beach, apprehending two Spanish pornography smugglers in a small boat, seizes 6,000 copies of 'Tits and Bums' and 4,000 copies of 'Shower Sheila', before fighting them to the death. The Spanish porn tide stemmed, for now, he rides home to find his wife, who is avidly reading a copy of 'Gay Boys In

Bondage' which, she explains, is Shakespeare's latest. This whole, lengthy saga then ends with a modern-day Sgt Maddox entering and arresting Gaskell / Sydney (if you follow!). Some superb Gilliam animated Tudor sequences have bolstered this whole piece enormously.

After this, we cut to Cleese and Cleveland as a young couple at a table outside a cafe, when Palin enters as a dishevelled looking vicar with a large suitcase, who asks if he can join them, but emphasises over and over again that he will only do so if it does not disturb them. As soon as he sits down he thanks them and immediately begins an insane display of smashing plates on the table, hitting a rubber crab attached to a table tennis bat, shouting bizarrely and spraying crazy foam all around. After his departure, it is clear that the couple have been converted to his way of behaviour, and head to his church, St Loony-Up-The-Cream-Bun-And-Jam, where shortly after they enter the whole congregation breaks out in a chorus of silly noise. Jones, the naked organist, appears and finally, after fifteen minutes, we have the opening credits!

Two short sketches follow. Firstly, there is a poor quality routine involving doubtful words in a telegram, which receives an apology for its extremely poor nature at the end, and then Cleese presenting a TV show called 'Is There?', debating whether there is life after death with his guests, three dead people. These two sketches are linked by a brilliantly imaginative Gilliam routine whereby the picture after the first sketch is folded up, put in an envelope, transported by horse then taken out and unfolded to reveal itself as the TV show scene. Considering the effects technology of the time, it is impressive. The strange episode title is finally explained in the next sketch, which begins with Palin as a man who says words in the wrong order (a typical Idle role normally) speaking to his doctor, named E Henry Thribshaw (Cleese), who declares that he is suffering from a new and undiscovered disease so fascinating that it will be turned into a film. It is, of course, and we see Cleese as Thribshaw discussing it with Chapman's extremely boring film critic.

Time for the final sketch now, with Chapman going to see a vicar who becomes obsessed with having sherry, and the rather flimsy premise of the sketch is brought to a head with him being revealed as the biggest customer of the British Sherry Corporation, along with 'The United States'. Spanish guitarists, dancers and a singer enter, performing a song in praise of Amontillado, the vicar informs the singer he wants some dirty magazines, and the credits roll with all concerned given a smutty pseudonym or description.

Comments.

If this episode seems somewhat padded out, especially in the second half, it is because three sketches originally intended for it were cut in their entirety. Two of these, one featuring revolting cocktails and another 'wee-wee' sold as wine, for their content and a third, about a long-nosed sculptor, allegedly owing to Chapman's poor performance. Some Gilliam animation was also cut. The 'Cocktails' sketch would later turn up on the *Live At Drury Lane* record.

The film representing the 'Thribshaw's Disease' movie comes from a 1960 Polish movie entitled *Knights Of The Teutonic Order*.

The Elizabethan girl encountered by Palin when he first enters the Tudor period is the first television appearance for Rosalind Bailey, who (unlike most *Python* guest stars!) went on to have a 30-year TV career, with her most recent appearance being in *Coronation Street* in 2012. She also appeared in good-sized roles in *Emmerdale*, *When The Boat Comes In* and *Poirot*, among many others.

The closing credits display all concerned with suggestive names and/or descriptions, which, of course, is in reference to the Tudor Porn sketch. However, the show title, listed as 'Monty Python's Flying Censored' is most likely to be a riposte to the BBC cutting two sketches for their content.

Author's Pick.
With the episode running out of steam after the halfway point, the strongest item is most certainly the whole Tudor jobs/porn saga.

Episode Eleven: Dennis Moore
First aired 4 January 1973
Sketches include:
Boxing Tonight
Dennis Moore
What the Stars Foretell
Doctor
TV4 Discussion
Dennis Moore 2
Ideal Loon Exhibition
Off-Licence
Dennis Moore 3
Prejudice
Dennis Moore 4

Synopsis:
First up here sees the guys training their sights on televised sport again, as 'Boxing Tonight' sees Jack Bodell pitted against art historian and broadcaster Sir Kenneth Clark. The muscle-bound fighter Bodell (played by stunt man, actor, boxer and bodyguard Nosher Powell) easily beats the septuagenarian knight of the realm with only a few punches to claim the title of Oxford Professor Of Fine Art. After the credits, we meet Cleese's highwayman Dennis Moore for the first time, as he stops a coach and horses, demanding they hand over their lupins. Bizarrely, he is vindicated as this does turn out to be the Lupin Express, and he seizes the concealed flowers. Moore races across the fields on his horse, Concorde, accompanied by his theme song, to present the lupins to a poor peasant couple before he bursts into a well to do country

house where learned historical matters are being discussed, and once again relieves the occupants of their hidden lupins. Riding away at speed again, he arrives at the same peasant cottage where he finds the man nursing his sick wife, wrapped in lupins, and trying to get her to eat something. Some lupins, that is. When Moore announces that rather than medicine, food or clothing he has brought lupins again, the man flies into a rage at how sick he is of bloody lupins. Even the cat has choked on them. He gives Moore a new 'shopping list' including money, jewellery, ornaments, watches, lace, a cat etc., and away goes our hero back to the grand house again, from which he returns with an enormous bag dragging behind his horse reading 'SWAG' on it.

After the peasants receive this bounty with joy, and we seem to have a happy ending, it's on to something, well, completely different. Idle and Chapman as two of the 'pepperpot' ladies are discussing horoscopes in the newspaper, looking up their star signs 'Derry And Toms' and 'Basil'. After some nonsense concerning foretold visits from Petula Clark, Peter Wyngarde, The Mike Sammes Singers and Duane Eddy's school friend, a doctor, played by Jones, is lowered from the ceiling. After shooting his medical bag in frustration after failing to open it, he robs them at gunpoint. They thank him, and we cut to a hospital ward where a doctor on his rounds is relieving the patients of all of their money.

After a televised debate about a fourth TV channel (a hot topic of the time) with four experts, which consists entirely of two saying 'yes' and two saying 'no', we are off to the 'Ideal Loon Exhibition', where we meet such eminent idiots as four Italian priests in custard, five dancing French osteopaths, a Marching Band Of Massed Pipes And Toilet Requisites, who are playing items of bathroom furniture, and finally the British loony, Chapman, who is lying suspended in two enormous tyres. Following some excellent Gilliam animation, including the old black-circle-becomes-a-hole joke, we see Idle delivering some earnest poetry before shopkeeper Cleese reminds him he is in an off-license. Idle explains he has 'caught poetry', and Cleese sympathises by saying that he, himself, used to suffer from 'short stories'. In one of the worst punchlines ever delivered, he is asked when this was, only to reply 'Oh, once upon a time...'

This quickly takes us back to the hapless Moore again, robbing the wealthy upper-class lords and ladies who are now down to their underwear and a few spoons. He takes the spoons, and races to the cottage, where the peasants, surrounded by now with opulence and art treasures, complain and demand he steal something decent for a change. The chorus delivering his song make him stop with the line 'He steals from the poor and gives to the rich / Stupid Bitch...', and he realises the flaw in his redistribution of wealth. A hugely controversial, yet satirically brilliant, sketch featuring Palin presenting a show called 'Prejudice', discussing the nation's favourite national, cultural and sexual bigotry, brings us back to one final bit of Moore, hijacking another coach and desperately trying to share the occupants' money equally between them.

Comments.

Jack Bodell was an English heavyweight boxer from Derbyshire who held the British and European championships during the 1960s. He retired in 1972. In the sketch, he is played by Frederick 'Nosher' Powell, a prolific TV stunt man who also worked as an actor as well as a bodyguard and, indeed, a boxer. Sir Kenneth Clark, his opponent, was a distinguished Art Historian and Broadcaster born in 1903. He was no relation to Kenneth Clark, the present-day British politician. He presented a BBC TV series called *Civilisation*, in which he did tend to wander around, hands in pockets, while talking – in a manner extremely well imitated by Chapman.

Derry And Toms (the star sign referenced) was a department store in London which closed its doors in 1972. The horoscopes quoted reference many real people, including singer Petula Clarke (whose song 'Don't Sleep In The Subway' was referenced in 'Election Night Special'); actors Peter Wyngarde (*Department S* and *Jason King*), Roger Moore and Tony Curtis; guitarist Duane Eddy; and finally The Mike Sammes Singers, a rather bland vocal group who provided music for numerous television programmes and films during the 1960s and 1970s, as well as somewhat surprisingly doing the backing vocals for The Beatles' 'I Am The Walrus'!

Author's Pick.

It has to be 'Dennis Moore', in all honesty. Age and familiarity may have blunted the brilliant left-field impact of the lupin robbery, but it is still masterfully done, and a perfect deconstruction of the whole 'steal from the rich and give to the poor' idea. Cleese has gone on record as saying that the only great things he contributed to the third series were 'Cheese Shop' and 'Dennis Moore'. He's wrong, but this IS genius.

Episode Twelve: A Book At Bedtime

First aired 11 January 1973
Sketches include:
A Book at Bedtime
Kamikaze Scotsmen
No Time to Lose
Frontiers of Medicine – Penguins
Unexploded Scotsmen
Spot the Looney
Rival Documentaries
Dad's Doctors

Synopsis:

This episode goes straight into the opening title sequence with no introduction at all. This is because there was originally a pre-title sketch which has since been removed. See below for details of this. Meanwhile, after the shock of the sudden opening, we go to Palin as the earnest reader of 'A Book At Bedtime', with Sir Walter Scott's *Redgauntlet* the book in question. Sadly, he almost immediately gets derailed by significant trouble reading some of the words. He is interrupted by an irritated and pompous Cleese, who starts loftily but then begins to struggle himself. So it goes from reader to reader, until a crowd form around them. This returns as a running gag, and by the end there is a large crowd, including a man carrying a stuffed flamingo.

Continuing the Scottish theme of Scott's work, we head to a castle where the Queen's Own McKamikaze Highlanders, the British Army's first kamikaze regiment, are training by throwing themselves from the battlements. This training regime has its disadvantages, however, namely that numbers have dwindled from 30,000 to twelve in three weeks. Cleese enters as an officer with an important mission for the regiment and addresses the training officer (Jones) about it. Unfortunately by the time he finishes asking for men for his mission there is only one left, a manic Chapman, repeatedly attempting to kill himself in a state of 'Itsubishi Kyoko McSayonara'. They manage to restrain him, and Cleese announces there is 'no time to lose', which Jones finds fascinating as he has never heard the phrase before. He struggles to use it properly, accenting all of the words wrongly, and we cut to a building signposted 'No Time To Lose Advice Centre', where Palin is a bowler-hatted man being taught by instructor Idle to use the phrase so that he has something to say to his wife. Unsurprisingly, he is struggling. An animation entitled 'No-Time Toulouse', featuring Toulouse Lautrec as a Western Gunslinger, cuts in helpfully.

With Chapman restrained, he is bundled into an army vehicle by Cleese and Jones but soon jumps out. They put him in the back and, in a tremendous, speeded up film scene, he repeatedly runs around to the front, lies down so it runs over him safely, runs around again, and so on. It's brilliantly timed. We leave his mission for now, however, as Cleese begins a scientific lecture about penguins, which posits the theory that penguins may be more intelligent than humans using utterly meaningless data put forward by Australian scientists who are repeatedly playing tennis. All that is proven is that penguins are more intelligent than BBC Programme Planners, and we see them firstly taking over the BBC boardroom and then important positions worldwide (Heath, Nixon, Prince Phillip etc). After we cut to the Kremlin, the mission is finally revealed, as Chapman hurls himself through a glass roof onto important documents. He is primed to explode and must be deactivated by the Unexploded Scotsmen Squad.

Next up, is an unrelated show entitled 'Spot The Looney', which should need no explanation. There are some very amusing lunatics, however. One of these is Sir Walter Scott, who puts the blame on Dickens. This cuts to Cleese as a clichéd reporter out in the countryside, walking with a microphone as he drones on about Scott. Palin appears as a rival reporter, steals the microphone and begins walking the other way, talking earnestly about trees. They begin stealing the microphone from each other with increasing violence until a high-speed car chase is the conclusion. They crash, the opening Scott book is finally finished, and the credits roll followed by a final sketch introducing fictitious new BBC sitcoms based around such familiar names as *Dad's Army* ('Dad's Doctor', 'Dad's Pooves'), *Father Dear Father* ('Limestone Dear Limestone') and the bizarre amalgam which is 'On the Dad's Liver Bachelors at Large'.

Comments.

The episode, as originally broadcast, began with a sketch called 'Party Political Broadcast (Choreographed)', in which political figures of their time put their points forward via the medium of dance. When the episode was repeated in 1979, during the run-up to the General Election, it was removed for fear of influencing the outcome. An odd thing to think, perhaps, but what is most surprising is that it has never been reinstated since. The closing 'Dad's Doctor' sketch was also removed for some considerable time, but that was most likely the BBC taking exception to some of their leading sitcoms being satirised, and it has been restored in recent times.

The 'book at bedtime', *Redgauntlet*, is a historical novel set in Dumfries in 1765, by Sir Walter Scott and published in 1864. It is highly regarded among his works. True to *Python* form, however, the passage being read does not actually appear in the book.

The three Australian professors in the 'penguins' sketch are all named after tennis players. Two of them are self-explanatory, as Ken Rosewall and Lew Hoad were both Australian and ranked number one in the world during the 1960s. The third one, however, Peaches Bartkowicz, played by Palin, is somewhat of a curveball, not least because she is female. Named Jane Marie Bartkowicz, and nicknamed Peaches, she was an American player, and her best Grand Slam finish was as Quarter-Finalist in the US Open in 1968 and 1969, so her inclusion is quite inexplicable.

The photo line-up in 'Spot The Loony' shows the following: Anthony Barber (Conservative Chancellor Of The Exchequer at the time), Katie Boyle (TV personality), Edgar Allan Poe, A Loony, Reginald Maudling (again), Tony Jacklin (golfer). One of the loonies in the sketch can be identified as Tarquin Fin-tim-lin-bin-whin-bim-lim-bus-stop-F'tang-F'tang-Olé-Biscuitbarrel, from 'Election Night Special'.

The phrase 'The Gathering Storm' is used for the second consecutive episode, this time as the subtitle of the investigation into penguin brains. 'The Gathering Storm' is the title of the first volume of Winston Churchill's six-part *History Of The Second World War*, published in 1928, so its relevance to penguins is sketchy at best.

Carol Cleveland is uncredited in this episode, but she appears as the Make-Up Girl in 'A Book At Bedtime', correctly reading the word 'Montrose'.

Author's Pick.

This is extremely close between the whole Kamikaze Scotsmen saga and the 'Rival Documentaries' sketch. Both contain brilliant sequences, but I will just narrowly give it to the Scotsmen, if only because it takes up so much of the episode, and forms its backbone.

Episode Twelve: The British Showbiz Awards
First aired 11 January 1973
Sketches include:
Thames TV Introduction
British Showbiz Awards
Oscar Wilde
Pasolini's Film: 'The Third Test Match'
New Brain from Curry's
Blood Donor
International Wife-Swapping
The Dirty Vicar Sketch

Synopsis:
This episode, the last one made by all six Pythons, opens with more TV boundary-pushing of the highest order, as the first thing we see is the actual identifying sequence for Thames TV (a region of the BBC's rival broadcaster ITV), with Radio DJ David Hamilton appearing to announce an action-packed evening on ITV, but now 'a rotten old BBC programme', followed by the usual intro to the credits... which do not follow. Instead the credits roll for 'The British Showbiz Awards'. Eric Idle introduces this with a typical performance as an obsequious host, gushing with fake tears and equally fake affection for the likes of David Niven (who has sent his fridge instead of himself) and the rest of the mostly non-appearing stars.

In between Awards links, we see the 'Oscar Wilde' sketch, in which Wilde, Whistler and Shaw attempt to first amuse the king with exaggerated witticisms, before trying to land each other in trouble by delivering insults ('Your majesty is like a stream of bat's piss'), and crediting it to one of the others. Next up after this is 'The Third Test Match', a film showing a cricket match as reimagined by Italian director Pasolini. The action is constantly interrupted by 'arty' images of death, sex and surreality, before the legendary director is cross-examined by a disapproving group of Yorkshire cricketers, complaining about, for example, the lack of references to Geoff Boycott's average.

Next up, the picture dissolves onto a television set in a living room, watched by Chapman and Jones in 'pepperpot' women guise. Both are named Mrs Zambezi. The Jones Zambezi is identified as needing a new brain, which they duly order over the phone from electrical store Curry's. A salesman comes and fits it – it simply sits on top of her head. He calibrates it, but she still often speaks in random words. They go out to give blood, and we cut to the blood donor department, where Idle plays a man who is desperate to give urine instead of blood. He eventually blackmails the doctor (Cleese) by stealing some of his blood. It's weak, and soon leads into 'International Wife Swapping', another sport pastiche as the sped-up film of comings and goings across a road is commentated as if a horse race, before a Rugby league match, commented on by Idle in 'Eddy Waring' voice, is seen, with Mrs Colyer used as the ball.

It's all very strange but leads into the end credits, which continue the wife-swapping theme by crediting all participants in various permutations, mainly with other people's wives. Finally, we see the final award which goes to the cast of the 'Dirty Vicar Sketch' which we see. It features Terry Jones as a dirty vicar in a historical setting who gleefully assaults two rather refined ladies. Announcer (Idle) comes on and weeps again, cast take a bow, and we fade out to 'The End'.

Comments.

This being the final 'Full Monty' show as we might say, there are a few self-referential moments incorporating previous scenes from the series. The 'dummy Princess Margaret' is in the Royal Box at the Showbiz Awards (along with the panto goose), Mrs Zambezi Two checks her shoe size when she talks on the phone, we see a penguin at a bus stop with two unexploded Scotsmen next to it, and finally Richard Baker is nominated for an award for his 'Lemon Curry?' remark.

The Rugby commentary in the Wife Swapping sketch is an impersonation of Eddy Waring, an English Rugby League commentator of the time who was regularly the target for impressionists. The trailer for 'Wife-Swapping With Coleman' on Wednesday evening is a reference to the midweek sports show *Sportsnight With Coleman*, presented by David Coleman.

Pasolini, the director of the 'Third Test Match' film, was an actual intellectual, 'arty' Italian director, known for such controversial works as *Arabian Nights* and *120 Days Of Sodom*. He died in 1975. The cricketers referred to by the panel, Geoff Boycott, Ray Illingworth and Fred Titmus, were all England cricketers. Boycott and Illingworth went on to further their stellar careers in TV work. Titmus, a half-forgotten Middlesex bowler who lost four toes in an accident with a boat propeller while on tour in the West Indies with the England team, was later immortalised in a song irreverently titled 'Fuckin' 'Ell, It's Fred Titmus' by the band Half Man Half Biscuit, which affectionately dealt with the surprise by a fan of seeing Titmus in ordinary situations. Definitely Pythonesque.

David Hamilton appeared as himself in the opening 'Thames TV' spoof.

During the 'New Brain' sketch, Cleese appears wearing a hat with a very prominent tag reading 'L.H. Nathan'. LH Nathan was a film costumier, who had, at the time, recently worked on *Carry On Henry*, but the significance – undoubtedly an in-joke – is unclear.

The two ladies in the 'Dirty Vicar Sketch' are played by Cleveland and Caron Gardner, who was herself a fairly prolific TV actress in mainly small parts from 1961 until 1984.

Author's Pick.
Not a classic episode in terms of individual sketches, I will plump for Pasolini's 'Third Test Match', narrowly above 'Oscar Wilde', as the latter has been done more effectively since, on stage.

Series Four
All episodes produced and directed by Ian MacNaughton

By the time the fourth and last series came to fruition in 1974, Cleese had finally done what he threatened to do after Series Two, and left the party – at least as far as television was concerned – as he stayed around for the films and the records, as well as various stage reunions.

In the two years since Season Three, there had been much activity on what had become the *Monty Python And The Holy Grail* film, after many false starts and changes of direction. Indeed, for quite some time the likelihood of a fourth series was heavily in doubt, as a result of concerns as to whether it could work without Cleese and subsequent drawn-out attempts to get him to stay. Idle was the most vocal in his doubts regarding the wisdom of continuing, though he ultimately agreed to give it a go. He did very little writing for the new episodes, however, and that side of things became very much dominated by Jones and Palin.

Owing to the work which was going on in 1974 to get the film finally completed, it was decided to do only six episodes, with an option to do a further seven later. Despite the new shows being quite well received, however, it remained at the six as Idle expressed his dissatisfaction very strongly after the series had been shown, announcing his opinion that it had been a failure, and deciding to leave himself. Like Cleese, he would continue with the films and records. Thus, after these six episodes, the 'Flying Circus' came in to land. The films would only ever use the *Monty Python* part of the name, with the *Circus* soubriquet applying to the TV incarnation only. So, *Monty Python* was dead – long live *Monty Python...*

Episode One: The Golden Age Of Ballooning
First aired 31 October 1974
Sketches include:
The Montgolfier Brothers
Montgolfier Brothers in Love
Louis XVI
The Court of George III
Party Political Broadcast on Behalf of the Norwegian Party
Zeppelin
The Golden Age of Colonic Irrigation

Synopsis:
This episode begins with Palin as a plumber, deep into his work on a toilet, delivering an introduction as regards the Montgolfier Brothers and their pioneering ballooning work. This soon cuts to the 18th Century, and Joseph and Jacques Montgolfier (Jones and Idle) are discussing their upcoming balloon flight plans. Talk soon turns to the subject of washing, as Joseph

reveals the trouble he has had washing properly for some time, with Jacques encouraging and advising him with altogether far too much enthusiasm for the subject. Chapman enters as their butler, announcing that a Mr Bartlett (who looks like a plumber) is here to see them. They refuse to see him, as they do throughout the episode.

We then cut to a BBC screen advertising the rest of the 'Golden Age Of Ballooning' series, along with an accompanying book and all manner of other worthless tat to accompany it. These are given with a price and a suggested prison sentence for not buying them. It is back to the next 'Ballooning' episode, and we see Joseph with his fiancée, Antoinette. She accuses him of being obsessed with ballooning, which he refutes, though his protestations are undermined that she is suspended horizontally off the ground hanging from a large airbag as he takes measurements. Jacques comes in announcing that he has run his bath, and the Butler again enters to announce the arrival of Louis XIV, which is surprising as he has been dead for several decades. Palin enters as the king, with two henchmen, a facial scar and a broad Scottish accent, and quickly amends his number to Louis XVI when it transpires that 14 and 15 are both dead. The Butler hopelessly fails to find the claret which he has been asked to fetch, as he requires directions to the sideboard holding the wine. Meanwhile the fake king, who clearly has no idea what 'Paris' is, takes the brothers' ballooning plans, headbutting Joseph along the way (who entered in a towel and a shower cap) with the so-called 'Glasgow kiss'.

Things seem to have taken another turn, as two extremely boring men speak on a TV discussion show called 'Discussion'. While they drone on, the presenter (Palin) directs us to the court of King George III sometime later. We go there, and see the French imposter announced as 'Louis XVIII', which gets rounded back down to XVI. He tries to sell the plans to King George, but Joseph again enters straight from the bath and denounces him as an imposter. Lord North gets headbutted as he announces the arrival of three black singers in modern showbiz dress who proceed to sing a song entitled 'George III'. We cut from this to six months later with Jacques making a play for Antoinette as they discuss the fact that Joseph is still missing ('he was only wearing a towel'), and the Butler enters to inform them that he is still searching for the claret. He then begins to receive rapturous applause, as people enter and present him with flowers as he takes a bow applauded by his fellow cast members. And there we leave the Montgolfiers.

But not the matter of hot air-assisted flight. Oh no, because after a short party political broadcast on behalf of the Norwegian party, we are introduced to the Zeppelin family, pioneers of the airship. We see archive footage of the least talented family member Barry Zeppelin, as he inhales from a balloon he is inflating and floats away, and then meet Ferdinand, who is being congratulated mid-flight in his airship by a host of dignitaries. Unfortunately, he becomes enraged when they persist in calling it a balloon, and he throws them overboard. They all land in the drawing room of a German couple, who are sitting reading a book about food. They identify the pile as being the government and proceed to arrange them neatly. We learn of a chain of events, beginning with someone killed by one of the falling ministers leading right up to the director of the 'Golden Age Of Ballooning'. Finally the titles come up for a new show, an adaptation of *The Mill On The Floss*. Part one is entitled 'Ballooning'...

Comments.
The vintage film of the unfortunate Barry Zeppelin was shot at Motspur Park in South-West London, as can be identified by the 'South East Gas' gasometers (gas containers) in the background.

Ferdinand Zeppelin has just two siblings, a brother and a sister. This differs markedly from the fourteen Zeppelin brothers referred to in the episode.

The butler introducing visitors to the court of George III is not mentioned by name in the episode but is identified in the script as Lord North, who was Prime Minister from 1770-1782.

The German couple whose roof the falling ministers plummet through, are clearly there to lampoon the perceived German love for order and organisation – they are reading an alphabetical list of food items, they bicker about the precise names for rooms and they arrange the dead government ministers neatly by job description.

The song 'George III' was sung by a trio of singers announced as The Ronettes, but are very clearly not. It was written by Neil Innes, in his first contribution to *Python*, and his biography on the Rutles website claims that it was actually performed by US group The Flirtations.

Palin wrote almost all of this episode on his own.

Author's Pick.
Not the strongest episode to begin the final series, but there are several good scenes. The trouble with this is that they rarely add up to a strong overall 'sketch'. The best sketch as a whole, is probably the whole 'Zeppelin' affair, with the film of Barry and the throwing out of the government ministers being very funny.

Episode Two: Michael Ellis
First aired 7 November 1974
Sketches include:
Department Store
Buying an Ant
At Home with the Ant and Other Pets
Documentary on Ants
Ant Complaints
Ant Poetry Reading
Toupee Department
Different Endings

Synopsis:

This is a return to the single-story 'Cycling Tour' approach for this second episode and a very successful one as well. It begins with a new opening title sequence (albeit with the familiar music), naming the show as simply *Monty Python* without the 'Circus' component, followed immediately by the closing credits. We start with a department store where Idle enters as a customer named Chris Quinn (via various visual gags such as people leaving with nose injuries after walking into the door, Palin's toadying doorman being kneed in the groin by a wealthy woman, etc.) and passes a customer (Carol Cleveland) trying out a flamethrower. Walking on, he passes a man whose coat is on fire, and reaches the 'Ant Counter'. After encountering two salesmen who both appear from behind the desk wearing a strange green rubber mask and gesticulating, it becomes clear that they thought he was Michael Ellis. This is the running theme, via tannoy announcements, television programmes and the like, but we never discover who Ellis is. After complaining to the manager, he announces that he wishes to purchase an ant, and chooses a mid-range one for one and a half pence. It comes with £148 of ant accessories, but he goes ahead and carries the huge box home.

Entering his house, we see his mother (Jones) gamely trying to give drugs to a large caged tiger, and filling food bowls marked 'Baboon', 'Dromedary', 'Gorilla', 'Trout' and 'Pangolin'. All are getting chopped meat. She is cynical about the ant, believing it will die 'just like the sperm whale', which he accuses her of not feeding properly, to which she quite reasonably asks where she was supposed to get 44 tons of plankton every morning. He goes through to watch television with the ant, who is called Marcus, on one of the many television sets which fill the room for no apparent reason. As luck would have it, the programme coming on is 'Ant Time', which is a sketch featuring Chapman and Jones as a waiter and customer who are human yet talking as ants, with grand gesturing of antennae and legs. Next up is a further ant documentary, which reveals that ants have six legs. Finding that Marcus has four, Quinn heads back to complain.

Finding the Complaint Department proves very difficult, and he is sent via the Victorian Poetry Reading Hall, where he finds such luminaries as Wordsworth, Shelley and Tennyson reading from their familiar works, changed to reference ants. Keats then rises and delivers a terrifying ode to an anteater before being bundled out. Then it is on to the Toupee Hall (where three very obviously toupee-wearing staff are in attendance) before finally, our hero finds the complaints department, which is immediately set on fire during a complaint about the flamethrower. Present are a man with one arm and trouser leg half the length of the other, a woman with a tennis racquet over her head, another woman with a pram which has a small column of smoke coming out of it, a man with a bandaged nose holding a dog with a bandaged nose, a man whose cigar has exploded and a lawnmower with a cat sticking out of it. We hear over the tannoy that 'Michael Ellis week has now finished and it is now Chris Quinn week'. He comments that this is a terrible ending, and is offered demonstrations of others such as walking into the sunset, a happy ending with a woman, a chase sequence (with *Dick Barton* music again), a slow camera pull-out, a summing up from a football panel or a fade to black. Which the episode does.

Comments.
A large portion of this episode was written by Cleese and Chapman, as one of the first submitted ideas for what became the *Holy Grail* film. Bizarrely, the man buying an ant was an early plot idea. If it had stayed in the script, the Knights would have found the grail and run into Chris Quinn, a historian, at Harrods.

A German girl in the department store lift was the first (uncredited) TV appearance for actress and model Suzy Mandel, who went on to be quite well known for a host of 1970s 'sexy comedies', such as the *Confessions* series, among others, throughout the 1970s. She also appeared in several TV programmes, such as *Benny Hill*.

The lift operator can just be heard announcing 'Fourth Floor – Kiddies' Vasectomies'. This was actually an overdub from the original line 'Kiddies' Condoms', which was considered beyond the pale even then!

The football managers being impersonated in the 'football panel' ending are Malcolm Allison (Palin) and Brian Clough (Idle). On the wall behind them is a photograph of Jimmy Hill, football player turned famous TV pundit, who presented the BBC show *Match Of The Day* at that time.

The 'Paisley counter' in the department store features not paisley patterns but rather people impersonating Northern Ireland Unionist figure Ian Paisley, much in the news at the time.

Author's Pick.
There are plenty of good candidates for the standout sketch in this excellent episode, with the house full of pets and the initial ant-buying scene hard to beat. However, I would have to give my vote to the tremendous physical comedy of Chapman and Jones in the ant/restaurant scene.

Episode Three: The Light Entertainment War
First aired 14 November 1974
Sketches include:
Up Your Pavement
RAF Banter
Court-martial
Film Trailer
The Public Are Idiots
Programme Titles Conference
Woody and Tinny Words
Show-Jumping
Newsflash

Synopsis:
The episode begins with a scene from a 'programme' entitled 'Up Your Pavement', with music based on the *Steptoe And Son* theme playing as two happy-go-lucky tramps walk up the road, stopping to search in a litter bin where they find a pie, a bottle of champagne and glasses. Straight away, though, they are run over by Alex Diamond: a TV hero in a sports car, who is a lumbago sufferer and patient of Dr Emile Koning: whose doorbell is just above Rear Admiral Humphrey De Vere, father of a young and inspired nurse who learnt the secret of Len Hanky: chiropodist, voyeur and hen-teaser, about whom the Chairman of Fiat once said 'what's a hen-teaser?' Yes Gino Agnelli, who once bought a telescope off a man who once stole a penknife from someone's brother's housekeeper's dental hygienist's uncle: The Reverend Charlie 'Drooper' Hyper-Hawk Swift!

After this crazed opening, we see Terry Jones as this fearless RAF Chaplain alighting from a WWII fighter plane, and we finally learn that this is the story of the men who flew with him. This takes us into the 'Banter Sketch', wherein each man who enters the small hut reels off a stream of typical wartime RAF banter, ridden with slang expressions. Each man is greeted by blank faces from everyone else, none of whom can understand a word they are talking about. A reference to German planes as 'cabbage crates' leads to a surreal discussion about how the enemy is trivialising the serious business of war by dropping cabbages instead of bombs, simply because they are cheaper.

This theme of trivialising the war, leads to a court-martial where Idle is a soldier standing accused of flicking wet towels at the enemy. Palin, prosecuting, is continually interrupted by the judge (Jones) who keeps demanding clarifications. One such is when Idle claims that Cole Porter was not the writer of the song 'Anything Goes'. Asked to clarify further, it turns out he is referring to an entirely different song which goes 'Anything goes in, anything goes out / Fish, bananas, old pyjamas / Mutton, beef and trout'. The sketch ends with a massed rendition of this song with all wearing pixie hats and big ears, accompanied by a roller-skating vicar.

Following this, is a black-and-white trailer for a war film, with captions such as 'Thrills!' 'Suspense!' 'Drama!' 'Marquetry', and a voice over-promising characters such as a 'half-man, half-woman parrot' and a 'half-parrot, half-man, half-woman, three-quarter badger ex-bigamist'. Next is a sitting room with Chapman and Jones as two 'pepperpot' ladies again, Mrs Elizabeth III and Mrs Mock-Tudor. A depressed 'punkah-wallah' servant figure (Gilliam in brilliantly lugubrious pose) stands by the television, which is showing 'Up Your Pavement'. They complain about repeats, press a button on a remote and Gilliam receives an electric shock prompting him to turn off the TV. One accuses the public of being idiots, adding that she herself certainly is, and a hilarious sequence plays out proving this. We then go to a BBC Programme Planner meeting, where they all suggest new programme titles, with Chapman, in particular, poking fun at his own writing for the shows *Doctor At Large* and *Doctor In Charge* by suggesting endless variants of 'Doctor At Three', 'Doctor At Bee' and 'Doctor Eats Cake'. Gilliam enters as a security guard in a wheelchair with a large sword sticking through his head ('Mind my war wound'), announces 'Trouble In Studio Five', and the 'Anything Goes' song comes on a TV set.

We now change to a period 'Agatha Christie' era room with Chapman, Cleveland and Idle sitting with servants standing behind them, having an utterly pointless conversation about words which sound 'woody', which are good, and 'tinny', which are not. Palin enters as one of the banter-spouting pilots, and again they fail to understand him. The pepperpots are, by now, happily watching footage of the M2, after which the electrocuted servant changes channel and show-jumping comes on. Marion Mould, the British Olympic silver-medal winning rider (for it is actually she) is on her horse, introduced by the announcer as 'Anneli Drummond-Hay'. She is jumping fences made of actual people, including 'The Sound Of Music', 'The Black And White Minstrel Show', 'Oklahoma' and 'Ben Hur'. Cut to the studio where BBC Newsreader Peter Woods reads a report about the British and German troops getting romantic with each other on the Ardennes front., and the madness is brought to an end by grainy footage of Neil Innes singing a romantic song 'When Does A Dream Begin' to an apparently disinterested young lady beside an aeroplane.

Comments.
The doctor in a surgical mask treating a lumbago patient in the opening sketch is, in fact, Douglas Adams, writer of *The Hitchhiker's Guide To The Galaxy*. John Cleese was originally nominated to play this part in the script.

The line 'Can't say "sodding" on the television' in the Programme Planners meeting is ironic (or deliberately self-referencing - who knows) since, in the series two sketch where Cleese designs an abattoir instead of a block of flats, he has to say 'oh (blows raspberry) the abattoir!' instead of 'oh, sod the abattoir!', which was ordered to be cut from the script.

The scene of Mrs Elizabeth III - with what looks like a weathervane on her head - in what was supposedly the car park below the Programme Planners meeting was actually shot from the roof of Clarendon House in Exeter.

The impressive grounds of what is announced as the Royal Arsenal Women's College, Bagshot is actually Bicton Park Botanical Gardens, in Devon.

The chaplain's fighter plane has 'Luke 17 v3' written on the side. This verse actually reads 'Take heed to yourselves: If thy brother trespass against thee, rebuke him; and if he repent, forgive him', and not, as it reads on the plane, 'Here we come Kraut'. He can be seen crossing off a German vicar's face as he alights. The aeroplane is a Hawker Hurricane Mk I, which is now on display at the Science Museum in London.

The girl to whom Neil Innes is singing 'When Does A Dream Begin' is Maggie Weston, the *Python* make-up girl who married Terry Gilliam in 1973.

The familiar pre-credit characters appear again here, but they are taken from previous episodes.

Author's Pick.
This is another episode with a lot of strong moments without a completely classic full sketch. Probably the best sketch overall is the 'Court Martial', if only for Palin's brilliant performance, but the most laugh-out-loud individual scene is Mrs Queen Elizabeth III's evidence that she is an idiot.

Episode Four: Hamlet
First aired 21 November 1974
Sketches include:
Bogus Psychiatrists
Nationwide
Police helmets
Father-in-Law
Hamlet and Ophelia
Boxing Match Aftermath
Piston Engines
Report From Epsom
Queen Victoria Handicap
Back To The Studio

Synopsis:
This time out we begin with the caption informing us it is 'Hamlet, by William Shakespeare'. However, we are greeted by a fast car screeching to a halt outside a large house. Terry Jones gets out dressed as a stereotypical Hamlet, black tights, crown et al. He enters the building and is next seen on a psychiatrist's couch, where he pours out his frustrations at having to keep doing the same old speeches, and wanting to branch out. The psychiatrist gets him onto the subject of sex, and as he gets excited leading to the question 'so, you've got her feet up on the mantelpiece...' he is bundled out of the room by another psychiatrist who apologises that the first one was bogus. This same thing happens several times, with every psychiatrist (and one policeman) reaching the same question being ejected. Finally, a computer is brought in, a huge cabinet thing with tapes. Predictably, it starts asking the same question and gets chased out of the room, where it runs with three pairs of legs sticking out of it. In the end, it is launched into the air in a field and shot with a bazooka by the nurse (Cleveland).

Next up is a spoof of the old BBC early evening show *Nationwide*, famed for its diverting if utterly unimportant news items. Idle, superb as presenter Michael Barratt, announces an item looking away from the small matter of World War 3 which has been declared that morning, and we cut to Chapman as a reporter named John Dull sitting in an armchair on Westminster bridge to look into how much better your legs feel when you sit down. A policeman (Palin) arrives to announce that the chair is stolen, but soon gets much more bogged down in the subject of policemen's helmets down the years.

On the other side of the bridge, we see Jones and Cleveland as a lovemaking couple discussing the fact that her father is going to live with them. However, as he has trouble getting to sleep on his own, she informs him that he is also going to share their bed. We cut to the three in bed. Father puts off the light and immediately sawing and hammering begins in earnest. Being pressed he informs them it is a model of the Cutty Sark which he has been making in the dark from wood for some time. They turn the lights on, and he is disappointedly holding some bits of wood randomly hammered together. Although, as he says, the sails are not yet attached.

After the credits, we cut to a bedroom where, after some odd banging on the wall routine we see the following in the bed: four Japanese businessmen with lapel badges, two American tourists with rain hats, three English gents with moustaches in pyjamas, four cyclists in full Tour De France outfits, three Swedish businessmen and Winston Churchill. In the corner of the room are bicycles. They are all tearful and eating popcorn, as they watch ... of course ... 'Hamlet'. We cut to the screen as Ophelia (Connie Booth), addressing Hamlet, reaches the question 'so, her legs are on the mantelpiece...' before she is bundled away by the psychiatrist's nurse.

Next up is the dressing room after a boxing match, The Killer versus The Champ, where The Champ is being carried in on a stretcher. They say it was a great fight and he almost had him, before mentioning a cut over his eye, and look at it on his head which is inside a paper bag quite separate from his body. The press are assured it will be stitched back on and there is no question of him being buried. The next item is a hospital ward where a room full of people are glued to a radio commentary where The Killer fights The Champ and knocks his head off while also punching a gaping hole through his body. However, The Killer is disqualified and the plucky headless Champ wins. They all cheer, a man having a heart attack is told to be quiet and doctors begin thumping patients.

It's a 'pepperpot' scene next, as several of them have been shopping and bought piston engines because they were 'a bargain'. One, Mrs Non-Smoker, is feeding the birds in the park by hurling food at them. However, rather than the more usual bread, she throws a leg of lamb, two tins of pineapple chunks, a jar of mayonnaise, a frozen turkey, a jar of onions, a bag of frozen peas and a bottle of wine. She buys a piston engine from Mrs Smoker and asks her how to cook it because, of course, you can't eat a piston engine raw.

We are approaching the end now as a series of sports studio items play, presented by Palin as former *Nationwide* presenter Frank Bough, including a report from Epsom by a dentist and a property developer, an interview by Idle with three jockeys who are so short only their hats are visible, and a look at the final race, the Queen Victoria Handicap, where we unsurprisingly see a set of identical Queen Victorias running around the course. Back to the studio and it is football as Idle, as Brian Clough, reports on a game in which a Real Madrid striker has been sent off for breaking wind. Ex-player and *Match*

Of The Day presenter Jimmy Hill then appears as himself, dressed as Queen Victoria, to explain about a Turin player who has been dismissed for having his living room knocked through. The presenter then turns to Hamlet, but asks him the obvious question and is bundled out of his own studio. A final scene has a company of Queen Victorias performing 'Hamlet', and the credits in full Shakespearean mode.

Comments.
This is the second time Jimmy Hill has appeared, although the other occasion was only in the form of a photograph on the wall of the studio.

One of the hospital patients listening to the boxing was played by an uncredited Reg Thomason. Never heard of him? Few have, yet he racked up a total of 179 small onscreen parts until his death in 2003. Most, like this one, were uncredited.

The third jockey interviewed, in the green cap and standing on the box, is thought to be Neil Innes, though this has not been confirmed. The Queen Victoria Handicap was actually filmed at Lingfield Racecourse.

The appearance by Connie Booth as Ophelia is her final *Python* role, and her first since Series three, Episode six. It is quite surprising to see her crop up in this final season, given that she was married to John Cleese at the time.

Author's Pick.
There is lots of excellent stuff here, as this oft-maligned final series continues to be very strong. The opening 'Psychiatrists' and the 'Father In Law' sketch are probably the picks, but Michael Palin's hilarious Frank Bough impersonation and the sight of Jimmy Hill appearing in the Queen Victoria outfit will be absolutely priceless to any UK viewers of a certain age!

Episode Five: Mr Neutron
First aired 28 November 1974
Sketches include:
Post-Box Ceremony
Mr Neutron
Teddy Salad
Secretary of State and Prime Minister
Mrs Scum
Teddy Salad Explodes
Conjuring Today

Synopsis:
Amazingly, this episode actually starts with the opening title sequence! *Python* must surely be the only programme where this comes as an actual shock. Anyhow, we begin with a normal suburban street, where a rag and bone man

shouting 'Any old iron' is rewarded by housewives putting things such as
missiles and rocket launchers onto his cart. Palin arrives with the mayor in a
Royal Mail van, and they climb onto a podium next to a post box, whereupon
he delivers a highly pompous and long-winded speech announcing the
opening of this new box. Then repeats it in French and German.

Bigger things are afoot, however, as we discover that the highly dangerous
Mr Neutron, a threat to the whole world, has arrived in the locality. We see
Chapman alighting from a train, with outrageous highlights in his hair and
wearing a hugely overstuffed yellow superhero costume with Mr Neutron
written on it. We are informed he is the most dangerous man on the planet
and then cut to where he is having tea in a garden with a couple called Mr and
Mrs Entrail. He makes small talk while Mr Entrail complains about everything.
Meanwhile in the USA, the Supreme Commander of the US military learns that
Neutron has gone missing and, while obsessively checking his own personal
hygiene (a running gag), he orders red alerts throughout the entire world.
Meanwhile, we see Neutron doing the weeding.

Over in the USA, the Supreme Commander orders Captain Carpenter up
to the Yukon to track down retired agent Teddy Salad, the only man who can
stop Neutron. The first hut he goes to contains a lumberjack who is fanatical
about ballet, and the second is an Italian restaurant set up by an Italian chef
from Oldham, who is getting very irritated by a party of Eskimos who insist on
ordering only fish, constantly. In the meantime, Neutron is hanging wallpaper.
Carpenter gets a lead from one of the Eskimos, who is MI6 and tracks down
a trapper on a sledge. After discussing ballet, the trapper points him toward a
dog, which is apparently Salad in disguise. Carpenter has to take the great ex-
spy for walkies.

Cut to England, where the Prime Minister meets the Secretary Of State in
an exclusive restaurant, so that they can discuss the US red alerts and nuclear
alerts, and the whole Neutron threat. Unfortunately, they are interrupted by
violinist Giuseppe, who, having mistaken the Secretary Of State for a woman,
begins playing a dreadful dirge called 'My Mistake'. This inexplicably causes a
conga line to form and gets so loud that the secret plans have to be shouted
at high volume. In the Yukon, meanwhile, the dog is starting to talk, but soon
needs walkies again. The US Supreme Commander, now naked behind his
desk and washing in a bowl of water, gives orders along with 'Moscow, Peking
and Shanklin, Isle Of Wight' that they will bomb Cairo, Bangkok, Cape Town,
Buenos Aires, Harrow, Hammersmith, Stepney, Wandsworth and Enfield. Which
they do. All by mistake.

Neutron, in the meantime, has fallen for Mrs Entrail's cleaning woman,
Mrs Scum, and plans to run away with her with the money he has won
in a Cornflakes competition. The net is closing though, as Salad, the
dog, gives Carpenter his address just as the Yukon blows up. Back at the
Supreme Commander's office, where he stands naked behind a vast array of
antiperspirants, we discover that the only places left unbombed are Ruislip,

the Gobi desert and his office. His office blows up. An animated sequence shows the world blown to pieces, as Idle, reading from the *Radio Times* (with *Python* on the front cover), lets us know that the story ends with Neutron's powers saving himself and Mrs Scum just as the last bomb falls on Ruislip. As the credits roll, he appeals the BBC to show us some of this thrilling acting, but instead, we see 'Conjuring Today', in which a mad-eyeballed magician (Palin) stands with a bloody saw about to cut a woman into three, before being chased off the set by police. Idle complains about this, and as we see him walking out of BBC Television Centre he is hit with a huge hammer.

Comments.

The *Python* guys have clearly still not forgotten about being cancelled for show-jumping coverage in series two, as another barb gets into the final scene, as Idle declares 'if you can put on rubbish like that, and the *Horse of the Year Show...*'.

Almost the whole of this episode was written by Palin and Jones alone. Oddly enough, the exception is the *Post Box Ceremony* sketch, which is delivered by Palin.

John Philip Sousa gets three different pieces of music used in this episode, with 'The Stars And Stripes Forever' and 'The Washington Post March' joining the familiar theme tune, 'Liberty Bell March'.

The name of the dog playing Teddy Salad is Bloopy. The only other credited guest role apart from the dog and Carol Cleveland is Bob E Raymond as an Eskimo, who actually appeared in all six of the final series episodes, yet none before. Douglas Adams again appears uncredited, as one of the 'pepperpot' women in the opening sketch. The mayor and mayoress are played by real-life married couple Len and Dot Webb.

The image used as the headquarters of FEAR (Federal Egg Answering Room) in the US is actually the Federal Reserve Board Building in Washington DC

The Eskimos use the name 'Anouk', but this is actually a Dutch name, not an Eskimo one. It is probably used because it sounds similar to Nanook ('Of The North').

The train from which Mr Neutron alights is in Lingfield, Surrey, the location of the Lingfield Racecourse, where the Queen Victoria Handicap was filmed. As he walks down the platform, he is carrying a small supermarket shopping bag from Sainsbury's, the famed British chain.

When Carpenter describes Salad as a 'hen-teaser', the man asking 'what is a hen-teaser?' in Italian is the FIAT chairman, in a clip from the third episode of this series.

Author's Pick.

The third full-fledged single-story episode, following 'The Cycling Tour' and 'Michael Ellis', this is not quite as strong as those two, but still contains some great material. Again, though, short scenes are the highlights (Mr Neutron in various household tasks, the talking dog, Palin's pronunciation of 'box' when opening the Post Box and his incredible eyeballs in the final sketch). Probably, the first Neutron sketch would get the nod overall.

Episode Six: Party Political Broadcast

First aired 5 December 1974
Sketches include:
Most Awful Family in Britain
Icelandic Honey Week
Patient Abuse
Brigadier and Bishop
Appeal on Behalf of Extremely Rich People
The Man Who Finishes Other People's Sentences
The Walking Trees of Dahomey
Batsmen of the Kalahari
BBC News

Synopsis:
The final ever episode of TV *Python* opens by promising us a Party Political Broadcast on behalf of the Liberal Party, but we are spared this fate and instead go over to the 'Most Awful Family In Britain' competition 1974, and the entry from the Garibaldi Family in Droitwich, current holders of the East Midlands regional award. Elements of their appalling home life include Gilliam as a hugely fat Kevin Garibaldi stretched out on the sofa with an overflowing plate of baked beans, constantly calling for more. His father sits at the table eating Ano-Weet cereal by the handful and discussing bowel movements in detail, while the other son Ralph keeps smashing random items up to and including the kitchen sink in sheer clumsiness. Mrs Garibaldi stands at the ironing board, where she is seen to iron the telephone, a lamp and the cat, all of which she hangs up flat. On the radio, we hear a football commentary in which all of the players are named Pratt. This fades out as Mrs Garibaldi irons it.

Cutting back to the studio, however, we discover that the Garibaldis are only third, and see a clip of the second-placed Fanshaw-Churneighs of Berkshire, who are all 'upper-class twits' who sit around the table talking very loudly and all at the same time. The winners are the Jodrells of Durham, who are so disgusting that we are not allowed to see them, but there are brief mentions of the grandfather's gobbing and Mrs Jodrell licking scabs off the cat. We cut to a family watching this on TV, who are as bad again, with dad wiping his feet on a loaf of bread, explaining that it is to get the 'cat doings' off, and the son eating corn-plasters. A cat is rammed through a hole in the wall by the door and is clearly functioning as the doorbell, screeching as someone pulls its tail outside. This is a man selling Icelandic honey for 'Icelandic Honey Week', before admitting that Icelandic honey does not exist. Meanwhile, throughout the episode, a puppet of a man wearing a yellow Liberal rosette keeps leaning into shot and waving at the camera – this is clearly intended to be then-leader Jeremy Thorpe.

Following this, we are into a doctor's surgery, where the doctor (Chapman) is interrupted by Palin entering gushing blood from his abdomen and complaining that he has been stabbed by the nurse. Chapman insists he fills a form in first and berates him for not even getting an easy question about the *Merchant Of Venice* correct. As he slumps to the floor, the nurse (Cleveland) enters, announcing that she has just shot a patient dead. As Chapman tells her off for this, she takes a long fencing sword and, after we hear screams, comes back to explain that there are no more patients. Palin is given another form to fill out while they go for lunch.

After a short sketch involving a pink tutu-wearing brigadier dictating letters to a bishop in a large mitre, we are treated to an appeal on behalf of 'Extremely Rich People Who Have Nothing Wrong With Them', and a man (Idle) who calls at the home of a woman who always has her sentences finished and teaches her to finish other people's sentences instead. As she then strides purposefully to Stonehenge for a bizarre link, we are in the jungle with a David Attenborough figure (Palin), sweating profusely and discussing the pursuit of the famed Walking Tree Of Dahomey. Not finding this, he instead stumbles onto some cricket-playing natives, the Batsmen Of The Kalahari. We then see footage of them playing against Warwickshire, killing several opponents as they bowl using fearsome spears instead of balls. The scoreboard shows us all of the Warwickshire players are named Pratt. Liberal-infused credits, a spoof news item and some link announcements later, and we fade to black and are gone. *Python* the TV show has run down the curtain and joined the Choir Invisible.

Comments.

This episode has two unusual outside-*Python* writing contributions, with Neil Innes writing the 'Most Awful Family' sketch and Douglas Adams the 'Patient Abuse' sketch, both in collaboration with Chapman.

The large skyscraper seen during the 'Rich People' appeal is Centre Point, a controversial 33-storey building which was completed after three years' work in 1966 and, absurdly, intended for a single tenant. No-one ever paid the asking price, so this enormous structure stood empty for almost a decade before being used as office space. As such it was a rallying point for homelessness protesters and activists.

The newspaper being read by Mr Garibaldi is The Scum (a spoof of the downmarket UK tabloid *The Sun*), and features a large headline about the weather and a woman's breasts, while the bottom the page informs us in smaller lettering 'China Declares War'.

The African nation of Dahomey (as per the fabled 'walking tree') would be renamed Benin a year or so after this episode.

The mention of 'the man to empty the Elsan' in the 'Awful Family' sketch refers to a kind of chemical toilet. At the time of broadcast, there was a recent

BBC TV programme called *The Family*, purporting to show a 'real' family, from Reading, in their home environment. This is generally accepted to be the source of the parody in the sketch.

As Jones walks to answer the door to the man who finishes other people's sentences, he can be heard singing the new 'Anything Goes' song from the third episode of the series.

The Icelandic Honey Week sketch was intended for the 'Michael Ellis' episode but was cut after ridiculous censorship arguments with the BBC. Incidentally, there actually is such a thing as Icelandic Honey.

The cricket match was filmed at Exeter Cricket Club.

During the end credits (which refer to all concerned in various degrees of Liberal-ness, and also with reference to make-up) a hesitant single guitar can be heard playing the familiar theme tune. This subtle but effective touch was provided by Neil Innes.

Author's Pick.
Not the best episode of this final series, but this does, however, have some strong material. The highlight has to be 'The Most Awful Family In Britain' sketch, which has become one of the best-remembered items from the final series.

The Films.

And Now For Something Completely Different.
Starring John Cleese, Graham Chapman, Michael Palin, Terry Jones, Eric Idle, Terry Gilliam
Also appearing: Carol Cleveland, Connie Booth
Directed By Ian McNaughton
Produced by Patricia Casey
Executive Producer: Victor Lownes
Released: 28 September 1971 (UK), 22 August 1972 (US)
Running Time 88 minutes

Less a film than a collection of sketches recreated on a meagre budget, this first, fledgeling step onto the big screen for *Python* was originally the brainchild of Victor Lownes, head of Playboy UK, who convinced the team that this would be the ideal way to launch them in the US. Seeing the logic in this, they went along with it but soon had reason to start regretting the decision, as Lownes proved unable to keep from interfering in the process. He began suggesting cuts and changes, at one point ordering one sketch featuring the Ken Shabby character to be cut out entirely, which it duly was. Not that his interference stopped there, as he crossed swords with Gilliam over the credits. As initially designed, Gilliam had the stars' names as blocks of stone, and Lownes insisted that his name receive the same treatment. Initially refusing, Gilliam was forced to agree, so he responded by redesigning the credits so that in the end Lownes was the only name given the stone treatment!

The film did quite well on both sides of the Atlantic, partly due to the fact that many UK viewers still had black and white TV, so this afforded them a chance to see the sketches in colour.

Synopsis:
Clearly, there isn't one, as this is a collection of sketches from the first two series, nothing more or less. Indeed, some people at the time did feel moved to comment that the very title was misleading, as this wasn't very different at all!

Nonetheless, there are changes worth remarking on, as many of these redone sketches are slightly rewritten, often for the best. The 'Mouse Organ', for example, now has the mice playing 'Three Blind Mice' (introduced as 'Three Blinded White Mice'), which works much better than 'The Bells Of St Mary's' in the original. 'Upper-Class Twit Of The Year' is streamlined and focused by cutting a couple of events, and the few spectators of the original are replaced by large stadium crowd scenes. 'Parrot Sketch' is followed by 'Lumberjack Song', which would go on to be the traditional arrangement, while 'Vocational Guidance Counsellor' has the would-be lion tamer Herbert Anchovy admitting that he just wants to see his name in lights, at which point Idle appears

115

dressed as a fairy, grants the wish, and he immediately appears as the host of 'Blackmail'. Arthur Pewtey is berated by the voice of God in 'Marriage Guidance Counsellor' rather than a cowboy, and the animation sequence of the prince with the black spot has the controversial word 'cancer' reinstated, rather than the (deliberately) clumsily edited 'gangrene' in the TV version.

Trivia.

The budget of £80,000 was so low that even some of the TV special effects were out of reach – which, given the general standard of British TV effects work at the dawn of the 1970s, speaks volumes. Much of the filming was done in the less than glamorous surroundings of an abandoned dairy.

The origin of the title phrase is generally credited to Christopher Trace, one of the original presenters of the long-running BBC children's show *Blue Peter*. He used to use the phrase on occasion to link items in the show, obviously entirely seriously at the time.

Monty Python And The Holy Grail.

Starring Cleese, Chapman, Palin, Jones, Idle, Gilliam
Also featuring: Carol Cleveland, Neil Innes, Connie Booth, Bee Duffell, John Young, Rita Davies, Avril Stewart, Sally Kinghorn, Sandy Johnson, Julian Doyle
Directed by Terry Gilliam and Terry Jones
Produced by Mark Forstater and Michael White
Released: 3 April 1974 (UK), 27 April 1974 (US)
Running Time 92 minutes

The 'real' film debut of the *Python* team first began life as early as 1972, when material began to be prepared with a partly historical, partly contemporary theme. By the time the film went into production in 1974, it had of course been rewritten several times over, with some of the rejected ideas being used for the fourth *Python* TV series. The budget of roughly £200,000 was much higher than the previous film, but still very low for a production of this type relying so heavily on location filming. It paid off, as the box office takings were roughly a dozen times that of the budget – and, of course, DVD sales ensure that the money still comes in today.

The Terrys Gilliam and Jones directed the film, which brought with it its own share of issues. Not only did they both have a steep learning curve, as neither had even directed a short film before, but also there was a certain amount of changing of 'sides'. Jones, in particular, had always been shoulder to shoulder with the others when resisting edits suggested by TV director MacNaughton, or the TV companies, whereas now he was in the awkward position of having to suggest some of the edits himself.

The film itself is rightly regarded as a classic, containing scenes which have passed almost into folklore, including The Black Knight, the French Taunter and the Knights Who Say Ni.

Synopsis:

Yes, there actually is a plot this time out. Opening in England, 963 AD, we hear the sound of horses' hooves over a hill, though what we are greeted with is King Arthur (Chapman) riding an imaginary steed, with his faithful squire, Patsy (Gilliam) following him knocking two coconut shells together. His first encounter is at a castle where his attempts to get the guards to ask their master to join him are foiled by a lengthy discussion about the non-ability of migratory swallows to carry said coconuts to England.

Next stop is a plague-ridden village where Idle is a mortician crying 'Bring out your dead' with a cart of bodies. After a discussion about him accepting someone who isn't, in fact, dead yet, Arthur passes by. He comes across a peasant named Dennis nearby, and once again fails to impress with his tales of Excalibur and the Lady Of The Lake as Dennis (Palin) belongs to an anarcho-syndicalist community, and lectures him on socialism. Finally, the first recruit is added to Arthur's party in the form of the slightly deranged Sir Bedevere (Jones). After encountering the Black Knight, and chopping all of his limbs off, Arthur comes upon Bedevere adjudicating in the matter of a witch accused by the villagers. He explains that as witches burn, and so does wood, they must be made of wood. Following this logic, wood floats and so do ducks, so if someone weighs the same as a duck they are a witch. The accused (Connie Booth) is weighed against a duck, matches exactly, and is found guilty. Following this, Arthur also recruits Sir Lancelot The Brave (Cleese), Sir Galahad The Pure (Palin), Sir Robin The Not-Quite-As-Brave-As-Sir-Lancelot (Idle) and Sir Not-Appearing-In-This-Film.

After an interlude wherein the party elect not to go to Camelot, as it is a silly place, they are greeted by an apparition of God in the sky, commanding Arthur to seek the Holy Grail. Filled with holy vigour, they stop at the castle of Guy De Lombard to ask him to join them but are taunted mercilessly by an astonishingly abusive guard. When this fails to drive Arthur away, they hurl a cow at the party, who respond by building a large wooden rabbit, but forget to get inside it and retreat. At this point, a modern-day historian appears to narrate some facts about the period but is immediately killed by a knight riding past. The police investigation into this forms a running joke throughout the film.

Now it is time to see how each knight fares after they split up to seek the Grail. Sir Robin encounters the Three-Headed-Giant but runs away while the heads argue among themselves, accompanied by his bard (Neil Innes), singing relentlessly about his cowardice in as many ways as possible. Sir Galahad meanwhile arrives in a fearsome storm at Castle Anthrax and is met by Zoot (Carol Cleveland) who informs him that the castle is populated only by 160 nubile young women starved of the attentions of a man. At first, he struggles, desperate to keep his vow of chastity, but when the offers become too tempting he decides he can stay for a little while. At that moment he is rescued by Lancelot bursting in and dragged away protesting vociferously.

Returning to Arthur, he is told by an old man to seek the Bridge Of Death.

This leads him first to the Knights Who Say 'Ni', who will only let him pass if he brings them a shrubbery. Heading to a nearby village, he chances upon a shrubbery salesman (Idle) and therefore manages to pass the fearsome 'Ni'-uttering Knights. Meanwhile, Sir Lancelot is with his squire Concorde, when Concorde gets shot by an arrow with a message asking for help being rescued. Believing this to be a damsel in distress, he instead finds, after murdering half of the castle, that it was in fact a somewhat weedy boy named Herbert (Jones) about to be married off by his father against his wishes. Finding this out, he apologises for murdering the best man but is still welcomed as an honoured guest by the ambitious father (Palin), who drops Herbert from the tower window and seeks to take Lancelot as his own son and bring the princess into the family. Herbert, however, has been mysteriously saved and Lancelot escapes.

Reunited, the knights meet Tim The Enchanter (Cleese) who warns them of a cave guarded by a most fearsome guardian, which they then underestimate when they see it is a rabbit. The killer bunny leaps at several of the party and rips their throats out before they retreat and manage to defeat it with the aid of the Holy Hand Grenade Of Antioch. Entering the cave, they see ancient writings directing them to the Castle Aaaarrgh, across the Bridge Of Death. After escaping an animated Black Beast because the animator drawing him has a heart attack, they reach the bridge, whereupon after some questions, Arthur, Lancelot and Bedevere make it across. They sail to the castle where the French Taunter is back to rebuff them again. Lancelot is seen being searched by the modern-day police looking into the historian's death. A huge army appears to ride to Arthur's aid and besiege the castle, when the police arrive in force, arrest the knights and stop the filming. The screen goes black.

Trivia.

Virtually all of the exterior filming (which is most of the film) was done on location in Scotland, with a great majority in and around Doune Castle in Stirling, though Glen Coe and the privately-owned Castle Stalker were also used. Plans to film at Hadrian's Wall were dropped owing to budget constraints.

The classic scene with the coconuts happened by accident, as real horses were originally planned. However, with the budget precluding this, they came up with the coconut shell joke as an alternative to get around the problem. Palin recalls in his diary that owing to these budget restrictions, the actors not only travelled by rented minibus but also had to drive themselves, which resulted in the odd sight of Lancelot and Galahad in full chainmail driving a 'Budget Rent-A-Van' around the streets of Stirling.

Chapman was suffering heavily from his drinking problems at the time, and one result of this was that he developed a severe fear of heights, which is not ideal when filming at the Gorge Of Eternal Peril. Indeed, Palin recounts that a severe attack of vertigo held up shooting the Bridge Of Death scene, on the very first day's filming. The Bridge, while appearing dangerous, was actually constructed by a Scottish mountaineer and was perfectly safe, but the assistant cinematographer had to cross as Arthur in Chapman's place.

In order to raise funds for the film's budget, ten investors chipped in £20,000 each. Three of these investments were secured from Led Zeppelin, Genesis and Pink Floyd. This was probably helped along by the connections of Tony Stratton-Smith, head of Charisma Records.

Elvis Presley was a huge fan of the film, and owned a private copy to screen at his Graceland mansion, and which he is known to have watched on at least five occasions.

There is a nod back to the TV series with Lancelot's squire, Concorde, which was also the name of Dennis Moore's horse.

According to Cleese, one of the funniest takes of the Castle Anthrax scene had to be discarded because a modern-day coat was visible in the shot.

The picture of 'Sir Not-Appearing-In-This-Film' in the credits is actually Palin's infant son, William, who is now Director of Conservation at the Old Royal Naval College, Greenwich – which surely makes anyone who remembers the film feel very old indeed!

The part of the policeman who stops filming with his hand at the end of the film is played by Julian Doyle, Production Manager on the film. The small non-speaking role of Dr Winston, one of the two nubile 'doctors' who try to minister to Galahad in Castle Anthrax, was an early on-screen appearance for Sally Kinghorn, who has since gone on to a wide range of roles including a major voice part in the animated film *Brave*. Her previous three TV appearances had all been as 'Maid'. The other attractive 'doctor', Dr Piglet, got all of the lines yet the actress, Avril Stewart, only went on to have two further TV roles.

The figure of God appearing through the crowd is in actual fact a photograph of 19th-century cricketer Dr W.G. Grace.

When The Black Knight has his first leg chopped off, the part where he has one leg was played by a real local one-legged man named Richard Burton (no relation!) because John Cleese had problems balancing on one leg.

When Arthur and the knights reach Camelot, the trumpet fanfare is actually the signature music of Rediffusion Television, who produced *At Last The 1948 Show* and *Do Not Adjust Your Set*.

The army at the end of the film is made up of 175 students from the University Of Stirling, who were paid the princely sum of £2 for the day. Among them was future writer Iain M. Banks.

During the scene with Bedevere and the witch, Eric Idle can be seen baring his teeth and biting the blade of his scythe. This was not an attempt to show his fury at the witch, but actually a way to stop himself laughing at that point.

Monty Python's Life Of Brian.

Starring Cleese, Chapman, Palin, Jones, Idle, Gilliam
Also featuring: Carol Cleveland, Neil Innes, Sue Jones-Davies, John Young, Spike
Milligan, Gwen Taylor, Terence Baylor, Kenneth Colley
Directed by Terry Jones
Produced by John Goldstone
Released: 8 November 1979 (UK), 17 August 1979 (US)
Running Time 93 minutes

Decades after its release, *Life Of Brian* is still the most remembered and
best-regarded *Python* movie – as well as the most controversial. Having gone
through writing sessions and script revisions for a couple of years, by the
time the finished article made its appearance in 1979 there had been several
Python-related projects featuring one or more of the group. Cleese had created
his legendary Basil Fawlty character in *Fawlty Towers*, Palin had made the
Ripping Yarns series (with help from Terry Jones), and Eric Idle had made
two series of his *Rutland Weekend Television* TV show as well as the Beatles
parody *The Rutles* with Neil Innes. On the big screen, the Gilliam/Palin film
Jabberwocky had come out to general approval. Getting the full gang back
together, however was – to use an extremely obvious cliché – the Holy Grail
for fans, and there was huge anticipation surrounding the film's release. This
eagerness was not shared by religious groups, whose objections to the film on
blasphemous grounds, while missing the point of the story entirely, provided
massive unintentional publicity. Clearly, the target of the film's satirical barbs is
the nature of belief and the issue of organised religion as a whole. The Pythons
have always asserted that, while the film can be looked on as heretical, it is
not, nor ever has been, blasphemous. Cleese even argues against the charge of
heresy.

  Shot on location in Tunisia, on a massively increased budget of some £3
million, there was a crisis when EMI Films withdrew backing from the picture
just before filming commenced. However, the day was saved by *Python* fan
George Harrison, who set up his company Handmade Films expressly to
enable the film to be made. He later said that he made this multi-million-pound
investment basically because he 'really wanted to see the film', leading Jones to
comment later that it constituted the most expensive cinema ticket in history!

  Direction this time was by Terry Jones alone, a move which was approved
by all of the other members. Chapman was again cast in the lead role, a
part which he wanted so much that he quit drinking and 'dried out' before
production began. Cleese had initially expressed interest in the role but later
agreed that Chapman was the best choice.

Synopsis:

The three wise men arrive at a stable, where a mother is with her baby. They
announce that they have been following a star, and bring with them gold,

frankincense and the less popular myrrh. Almost immediately, however, they snatch these gifts back as they realise that the saviour is actually in the stable next door. Thus begins the story of the 'reluctant prophet', Brian.

Brian Cohen (Chapman) is actually an ordinary chap, though secretly half-Roman, who we see after the credits watching Jesus deliver the Sermon On The Mount from a great distance away, with his mother (Jones). They head next for a stoning, which is promised to be a good one, featuring a 'local boy', and Brian's mother buys some rocks and also a false beard, as women are prohibited. At the stoning, Cleese, as the High Priest, announces the charge of blasphemy, accidentally utters the word 'Jehovah' himself, and is crushed by a huge rock. Brian becomes embroiled with the People's Front Of Judea, who include a young woman named Judith, with whom he has become very enamoured, and proves his credentials by daubing anti-Roman graffiti on the walls. Accepted into the group, Brian is arrested after a hopelessly incompetent plot to kidnap Pilate's wife, and after escaping (with the help of a bizarrely passing spaceship!), he finds himself standing on a podium where people address the crowds. At first, being heckled, he somehow ends up being taken for a messiah and is then chased into the desert by a baying crowd bent on worshipping him.

Ultimately making it back to his house, he has attracted a huge crowd outside, demanding that he address them. His mother fails to disperse them (despite the now-famous line 'He's not the messiah, he's a very naughty boy!', and in desperation Brian tries to convince them he is no leader or prophet. He sneaks out the back way, but is captured and taken to be crucified. The crowd demand that Pilate release him, which he agrees to, but when the order arrives another prisoner (Idle) claims to be Brian as a joke, and is released instead. The People Front Of Judea arrive, but merely applaud Brian on a splendid martyrdom, while their sworn rivals The Judean People's Front, send a crack suicide squad, who uselessly kill themselves in a gesture of solidarity. Finally, as the prisoners are on the crosses, another prisoner played by Idle (Mr Frisbee) begins the immortal song 'Always Look On The Bright Side Of Life', and the film ends with them all joining in, tapping their feet on their crosses, as we fade to black.

Trivia.
An early proposed idea for the film was to be about St Brian, the 13th Disciple, who attempts to be a gospel chronicler but is late for every major event, including the Last Supper because his wife has invited dinner guests. One proposed scene had Brian renting out fishing boats on the Sea of Galilee when Jesus is seen in the background walking past on the water. At this point the film was to be titled 'The Gospel According To St Brian'. One imagines that this may have caused even more opposition than the storm of protest which the finished product attracted, with Cleese notably commenting that they had managed to get the various Christian denominations to agree on

something for the first time in two thousand years!

The original cut of the film ran to two and a quarter hours, and it was suggested to leave it as it was, but it ended up being edited down by over 40 minutes. Scenes cut were the kidnap of Pilate's wife, an opening scene with shepherds who miss the star as they discuss sheep, and also a whole subplot involving the Judean People's Front and their leader, Otto The Nazarene, a hard-line Zionist with a Hitler moustache. This latter character originally appeared throughout, but was cut for the double reason of apparently slowing down the flow of the film, but also for reasons of not offending any more people! With a symbol resembling a swastika crossed with a Star Of David, this latter claim does have some merit! Gilliam later commented that they should have left it in as, having offended every Christian denomination in the world, 'we might as well have gone for the Jews as well'.

The filming took place on location in Tunisia. One major reason for this was that they were able to reuse locations from Franco Zefferelli's recent epic *Jesus Of Nazareth*, also filmed there. At the time of filming, it was discovered that Spike Milligan happened to be in Tunisia on holiday, and he was asked if he would like to take a cameo role, which he duly did, as a prophet who is ignored as his acolytes furiously chase Brian. George Harrison also appears briefly as Mr Papadopolous, owner of The Mount, who shakes hands and says hello to Brian.

During Brian's fleeing from the pursuing Romans, there is a bizarre CGI scene from Gilliam whereby he is rescued from falling to his death from a tower by a passing spaceship, which then takes part in some *Star Wars* inspired battle scenes before crashing to earth, allowing Brian to alight unharmed. The clear homage to *Star Wars* was justified later when George Lucas met Gilliam and made a point of praising his work on the scene.

The film was banned for eight years in Ireland, but it is less widely known that it was banned for a year in Norway. In fact, this was capitalised upon by an advertising campaign in Sweden which included the line 'so funny, it was banned in Norway!' Interestingly, in 2008 it was reported that a thirty-year ban on the film in Aberystwyth, Wales, had been lifted, and Palin and Jones attended the subsequent screening, along with the then-mayor Sue Jones-Davis, who played Judith in the film. However, reports that she had personally lifted this ban were revealed to be false when it was discovered, shortly before the screening, that the original ban had only been discussed by the council, and that the film had actually been scheduled to be screened in 1981. A self-perpetuating myth kept this so-called 'ban' in place for almost three decades! The Irish film censor, named Frank Hall, described the film memorably as 'offensive to Christians and to Jews as well, because it made them appear a terrible load of gobshites', which is surely the best line never to appear in an episode of famed Irish priest-based sitcom *Father Ted*!

Kenneth Colley, who plays the role of Jesus at the beginning o the film, had appeared with Palin in the *Ripping Yarns* episode 'The Testing Of Eric

Olthwaite'. Cleese originally wanted George Lazenby to play the role, and he wanted the film to have the tagline 'George Lazenby IS Jesus Christ!' Unfortunately, Lazenby was on another project at the time and unavailable. The part of 'Mrs Big Nose' (the wife of an Eric Idle character) was played by prolific UK television actress Gwen Taylor. Becoming very well known later for such programmes as *Duty-Free, Coronation Street* and *A Bit Of A Do*, she had appeared with Idle in both *Rutland Weekend Television* and The Rutles movie *All You Need Is Cash*.

In the scene where Brian appears naked on his balcony, Terry Jones made the comment after the first take 'well, I think we can all see that you're not Jewish', referring to his very much uncircumcised state. Subsequent takes saw this addressed with a rubber band, of all things!

The snacks that Brian is selling at the Colosseum when he meets The People's Front for the first time include Wolf Nipple Chips, Dromedary Pretzels, Jaguar Ear Lobes, Tuscany Fried Bat, Ocelot Spleens, Larks' Tongues, Wren's Livers and Otters' Noses. This menu would have been impossible as the jaguar and the ocelot were unique to the Americas, and were unknown to that part of the world, and indeed Europe, until over 1600 years later. Then again, there was no Colosseum or similar amphitheatre anywhere near Jerusalem either!

The newly-sober Chapman was so focused and together at this time that he also acted as a sort of on-set doctor, using his medical training to hold daily clinics for cast and crew.

The line uttered by Idle during the final scene, 'Bernie, I said, they'll never make their money back', is a very pointed jibe in the direction of Lord Bernard Delfont pulling EMI out of financing the film on the eleventh hour. That must have stung greatly after twenty million pounds had been grossed!

As is often the case with *Python*, several characters are named in the script without any mention of these names on-screen. Two of these are Eric Idle characters. His running character who jokes about being given freedom and eventually does gain that freedom after joking about being Brian is never actually referred to by name as Mr Cheeky. His character who sings 'Always Look On The Bright Side Of Life' is oddly named Mr Frisbee III, and Palin plays a guard referred to in the script as Nisus Wettus.

Idle's character in the People's Front who wants to be a woman named Loretta took that name as a reference to his friend Marty Feldman's wife, Lauretta Sullivan. The part of Judith was originally offered to Diana Quick after an audition, but she had to turn it down due to other commitments. She had appeared with Palin in the pre-*Python Complete And Utter History Of Britain*. Maureen Lipman and Judy Loe (mother of actress Kate Beckinsale) also auditioned unsuccessfully for the role of Judith. It seems slightly surprising that Carol Cleveland did not get offered the role – she has two parts in the film, but in smaller roles as Mrs Gregory and one of Brian's adoring crowd.

Monty Python's The Meaning Of Life

Starring Cleese, Chapman, Palin, Jones, Idle, Gilliam
Also featuring: Carol Cleveland, Simon Jones, Patricia Quinn, Judy Loe, Andrew
MacLachlin, Mark Holmes, Valerie Whittington
Directed by Terry Jones
Produced by John Goldstone
Released: 23 June 1983 (UK), 31 March 1983 (US)
Running Time 90 minutes

Arriving four years after *Life Of Brian* (the same gap as that came after *Holy Grail*), *The Meaning Of Life* was certainly an event much anticipated by fans and media alike, but in a slightly different way than the previous films. Whereas those two productions were hailed as important works in the development of *Python* (and in the case of *Brian*, almost a rebirth), *Meaning Of Life* always had a sense of finality about it. The participants knew it would be the last *Python* movie, and the rest of the world seemed to have tapped into that same feeling.

Nevertheless, despite being a return to the 'sketch' format rather than the fully developed narrative of the previous films, *Life* does contain more than its fair share of classic quotable *Python* moments and very funny scenes. 'One more wafer-thin mint?' is surely challenging 'he's not the messiah...' as the most quoted *Python* film line. On this occasion, the break between films had not seen as many side projects, with the most notable exception being Gilliam's *Time Bandits*, co-written with Palin and also featuring an appearance by Cleese. Indeed, Cleese (*The Great Muppet Caper*, *Privates On Parade*) and Palin (*The Missionary*) had been the busiest in the intervening years, with Jones, Idle and Chapman appearing in relatively little of note. Chapman's 'folly', *Yellowbeard*, was released at a similar time to *Meaning Of Life*, but it was widely condemned as being very poor, even by some of its stars.

When *Meaning Of Life* was released in cinemas, it was preceded by a 16-minute Gilliam-helmed support feature called *The Crimson Permanent Assurance*, a surreal accountancy/piracy hybrid wherein a building full of put-upon accountants launch their office building for adventure on the 'Accountant Sea'. Originally planned as an animated sequence in the main film, it was cut out, and Gilliam persuaded the others to allow him to carry on and make it as a live-action short. It is inessential. Note that a reference to the feature, in the form of a 'boardroom battle' does make an appearance during *Meaning Of Life*.

Synopsis:
We open in a fish tank. Yes, we do. The six fish have the faces of the *Python* team, discuss the upcoming film, and lead us to 'Part One: Birth', which is in two parts. Firstly Cleese and Chapman play two doctors delivering a baby while far more focused on their hospital equipment, including one very expensive machine which 'goes beep'. The second, and more celebrated, part of this first chapter sees a Roman Catholic family in Yorkshire (described as 'the

Third World') with the man (Palin) coming home to his house full of countless children, filling cupboards and the like, while the latest drops out of his wife (Jones) while she works at the sink. He has lost his job at the mill, and while there is a tremendous ensemble rendition of the song 'Every Sperm Is Sacred', he nonetheless has to inform his children that he has to sell them all for medical experiments. Chapman's protestant man across the road delights in this, revelling in the fact that he could use a condom 'or even a French tickler' whenever he wished.

Schooldays are next, as the schoolboys in church are followed by Cleese's classic sex education lesson, making love to his wife on a four-poster bed at the front of class while bored pupils lose concentration and look out of the window. The third chapter, 'Fighting Each Other', has three war scenarios, beginning with a WWI officer in the trenches shamed into setting a table to eat a cake that his men have made for him above their trench. All of the men are shot during this. A drill sergeant who allows all of his men to get away without their duty leads to the best part of this segment, a scene from the Zulu wars where Idle is an officer who has had his leg bitten off during the night but is making the best of it. A tiger, which is repeatedly commented on as not being from Africa, is blamed.

After a brief 'middle of the film' sketch featuring a surreal 'find the fish' routine, a 'Middle Age' chapter begins with a restaurant where conversation choice can be ordered from the menu, and then a 'Live Organ Transplant' in which an organ donor (Gilliam) is forced into donating his liver while he is still alive. 'The Autumn Years' are around the corner and take the celebrated (and revolting) form of Mr Creosote, the enormous man played by Jones, who enters a restaurant, vomiting into a bucket continually, while ordering and eating everything on the menu. Persuaded by waiter Cleese to have 'one more wafer-thin mint', he duly explodes.

Finally, we have the multi-part 'Death' chapter, begun by Chapman as a condemned man allowed to choose the manner of his execution, and accordingly being chased off a cliff by a group of topless women. There is a clever animation about suicidal autumn leaves before the grim reaper visits a rather well to do dinner party and claims all of the guests, who have unwittingly eaten the salmon mousse. They go to a sort of heaven where it is always Christmas, and they are serenaded by a ghastly collection of lounge-crooner clichés performing 'Christmas In Heaven'.

Trivia.

The sketch with the 'Every Sperm Is Sacred' song, despite being set in Yorkshire, was actually filmed in Colne, Lancashire – which probably had the good Lancastrian citizens of Colne up in arms when they recognised it. Palin considered the sensibilities of the children when he changed one line to 'rubber thing on the end of my sock', then dubbed in the word 'cock' later. Many of the children have commented since that they had no clue what they were singing about. Note (we count so that you don't have to): when they are sent off to be sold for experiments, watched by the protestants over the road, 64 children trudge out of the doorway and down the street. Many of these were the same child twice, however, as they came around the back and walked out again.

The surreal and rather creepy 'Find The Fish' was intended to represent the sort of unnerving dream that most people have from time to time. Gilliam has said that he wishes it had been better explained as such. It was filmed in the main hall at Battersea Power Station in London, and the green elephant head was a leftover costume from *Time Bandits*.

The 'Mr Creosote' sketch was filmed in the rather grand surroundings of Porchester Hall, a Grade II listed building in Bayswater, West London. There was something of a scramble on the final day of filming when vast quantities of fake, yet unpleasant, vomit had to be cleaned up ahead of a wedding taking place later on that same day.

The increasingly ambitious production of the short 'Crimson Assurance' film meant that it became the only *Python* film ever to go over budget, despite being only 16 minutes long! The feature included the debut performance from Matt Frewer, best known for being the original Max Headroom on TV in the '80s, and also having a major part in the series *Orphan Black*. He also played Pestilence in two episodes of *Supernatural*. Palin and Gilliam have cameo roles as window-cleaners.

Just before the film's completion, Douglas Adams published a book entitled *The Meaning Of Liff*, comprised of new words for things which haven't been invented yet, all of which are place names (for example, Kettering is defined as the pattern imprinted on the skin after sitting naked in a wicker chair). After he called Jones to explain about his book, the credits of the *Python* Film were designed so that a huge stone tablet at first reads 'The Meaning Of Liff', until a bolt of lightning adds the extra line to change the final F to an E.

Bizarrely, at the British Academy Film Awards that year, 'Every Sperm Is Sacred' was nominated as the best original song. Normal service was restored when 'Up Where We Belong' from *An Officer And A Gentleman* won the award, but how gloriously subversive, and utterly Pythonesque, it would have been, if the *Python* song had actually won...

After being turned down for the role of Judith in Life Of Brian, Judy Loe actually got to appear in The Meaning Of Life. Her excitement may have been contained, however, by her part being 'Nurse No 1'... Also, after only two relatively small roles in Life Of Brian, Carol Cleveland gets five different parts here, although two of them are voiceovers for leaves.

In the final scene, Graham Chapman is the first to open the door to Death, and the first to speak to him. He became the first *Python* to die a few years later, which is a little chilling. Palin's line towards the end, 'Hey, I didn't eat the mousse!' is a spur of the moment ad-lib which is not in the script.

Cleese had food poisoning while filming the Tiger sequence, and had to go out to vomit in between takes. It is probably as well this wasn't the Mr Creosote scene.

Jane Leeves (who went on to stardom as Daphne in the sitcom *Frasier*), makes her film debut in the 'Christmas In Heaven' number. One of the topless running girls was Nikki Diamond, a glamour girl who went on to become well known as Scorpio in the programme *Gladiators*.

The Monty Python Record Albums.

Monty Python's Flying Circus
Personnel:
Chapman, Cleese, Palin, Jones, Idle (Gilliam is omitted from the credits)
Also appearing: Carol Cleveland, The Fred Tomlinson Singers
Record Label: BBC Records (UK), Pye (US)
Recorded May 1970, produced by Ian MacNaughton.
Incidental Music by Anthony Foster
Extra Sound Effects by Hilary Morris
Release date: November 1970.
Running time: 53:13

Album facts:
This entry into the recording world for the Pythons is something of a half-hearted affair. That is not to say that the content is necessarily lacking, but the creative support and imagination shown by the BBC was found by the team to be very disappointing. This album, therefore, would be the first and last released on the BBC's own record label.

The recording was done in one day, in the late afternoon of 2 May 1970 at the Camden Theatre, London. A small theatre owned by the BBC at the time in the Camden area of London, it later reopened in 1979 as a live music venue called the Music Machine, as which it is arguably better remembered. It later became the Camden Palace before closing again and is now a nightclub named Koko. The audience reaction on the album is in places very muted, and led Idle to comment that as an audience they were 'particularly dead'.

As part of their cost-cutting measures, the BBC would only record the performance in mono. In one sketch, at the opening of the second side, Chapman demonstrates the stereo effect by walking from one speaker to the other – an effect rendered utterly useless by the BBC's decision. The rights to the album are still retained by the BBC, making it something of an odd album out in the *Python* collection, and as such it has not been included in any of the repackaging 'special edition' releases afforded to the later material on Charisma Records.

Album Cover:
Designed by Gilliam, the album cover is nevertheless rather bland and uninspiring, merely showing the rather predictable animated foot inside a TV screen. Certainly, there seems much less effort and imagination put into the design and packaging than the increasingly wild flights of fancy that the team were to indulge in after their move to Charisma. The rear cover was a plain text affair, featuring a short note from series producer Ian MacNaughton and a selection of reviews of the TV show (positive, of course). There was also a track listing, a feature which was abandoned with the next record. There is a small

element of humour on the reverse with the title amended to 'The Worst Of Monty Python's Flying Circus', but the overriding feeling is that the BBC were stuck a decade earlier when it came to record packaging, and also that they had little clue how to market what they had. This was not a regular comedy album.

Note: the cast of performers, clumsily appended to the bottom of the front cover, manages to misspell Graham Chapman's name as 'Grahame' and also omits Terry Gilliam from the performers despite his appearance in 'The Visitors'

Material.
Essentially, this was what the BBC had ordered: a selection of the best sketches from the first series of the show. However, even at this early stage in the relative creative vacuum of the BBC Records environment, the Pythons had more imagination than that. Several sketches are changed, either to run better or to translate to audio more effectively, and there is also a small amount of brand new material. Notable changes are Palin's homicidal barber (explanatory voice-over and removal of the 'tape recorder' gag which would fail to work in audio), the Frenchmen at the end of 'Flying Sheep' (shortened with an extra coda then added) and the 'Mouse Problem' sketch, which omits much of the fly-on-the-wall party footage. Palin also replaces Jones as 'The Man With Three Buttocks' for some reason. Brand new material includes the aforementioned test-your-stereo Chapman bit, a reference by Idle to Cleese as the interviewer 'from the other side' and some padding near the end of the second side, supposedly to fill up the running time. All in all, it added some freshness to the familiar originals and, in the home video-free world of the 1970s, the only way to relive this classic material.

Another Monty Python Record
Personnel:
Chapman, Cleese, Palin, Jones, Idle, Gilliam
Also appearing: Carol Cleveland, The Fred Tomlinson Singers
Record Label: Charisma (UK), Buddah (US)
Recorded June 1971, produced by Michael Palin and Terry Jones.
Release date: October 1971 (UK), August 1972 (US).
Chart Position: 26 (UK)
Running time: 45:45 (UK), 54:39 (US)

Album Facts.
After their dissatisfaction with the way the BBC handled their first album, the team were delighted to be offered a recording contract with Charisma Records in the UK and threw themselves enthusiastically into the creation and recording of this second record. Run by the eccentric yet widely admired Tony Stratton Smith, Charisma were one of the most quirky, 'progressive' and

determinedly 'English' of the record labels of the time. With early releases coming on a very collectable pink label bearing the legend 'The Famous Charisma Label', it was home to bands such as the fledgling Genesis and Van Der Graaf Generator, and quickly carved a niche for giving its artists a fairly long leash in terms of artistic freedom. This was perfect for the *Python* team, who were constantly pushing the boundaries of the BBC on the TV show.

The album was recorded over the space of five days in June 1971 at the Marquee Studios in London, and was produced by Jones and Palin who, are keen to perform the task. However, they soon found it a steep learning curve, with the amount of tape available resulting, before long, in hours and hours of unlabelled tape with the two having no idea of what was where. Jones also remembers some of the recording staff being clearly under the influence of certain relaxational substances at the time, and this not helping them get to grips with the new technology. Nevertheless, the production is innovative, with its extensive use of effects and such.

The US release came out the following year, in 1972, but was worth waiting for as it contained almost ten minutes of extra material which had been cut from the UK release, citing the limits of the vinyl format as the reason. This was subsequently restored to future CD pressings.
The album actually reached Number 26 in the UK album charts – an astonishing feat for a spoken-word comedy release, and proof positive of the 'rock and roll' appeal of the Pythons. This was a long way from sparsely-packaged, budget prices releases of Tony Hancock shows and other comedy artists at the time. Comedy had changed forever.

Album Cover.

The cover of the album – designed by Gilliam, from an idea by Jones – featured a classical record cover for Beethoven's *Second Symphony in D Major*, by the National Philharmonic Orchestra. This was hastily crossed out in black crayon with the words 'Another Monty Python Record' scribbled in alongside. This same motif was carried on to the spine and, on the original UK pressing, the record label (this first pressing mistakenly listed the year as 1970 on the label). The rear of the album continued the theme, with a lengthy, and apparently serious, essay about Beethoven. Reading this, however, reveals more and more references to tennis and, in particular, Beethoven's first appearance at the Wimbledon Championships, cropping up in the text. There is also a column about the making of the album and the credits, supposedly written by Stanley Baldwin.

Giving ever more vent to their creative ideas, UK copies of the album also came with a 'Be A Great Actor Kit', referring to a sketch on the second side. This consisted of a script, detailed instructions and cut-out props to accompany the sketch. All of this was a world away from the basic 'foot in the TV' design of the debut. The Pythons were 'home'.

Material.
The material on the album largely drew from sketches included in the second series of the show, but with quite a lot of original material as well. Introducing the album is a series of apologies around the nature of the recording, as it is mistakenly introduced to be a record entitled 'Pleasures Of The Dance', a collection of Norwegian carpenters' songs. Extracts from this fictitious record are included and then apologised for. One sketch, 'Stake Your Claim', featuring guests on a TV show trying to back up outlandish claims, is an English language version of a sketch which appeared on the first of two German *Python* Shows, *Monty Python's Fliegender Zirkus*. Sketches such as 'The Spanish Inquisition' are notably rewritten, and the infamous 'Undertaker' sketch is included without the intrusive audience 'outrage'. One excellent use of the medium, which rather lost its potency when any other format than vinyl was used, came at the end of the first side when, during the 'Piranha Brothers' sketch, the announcer is warned to truncate it immediately. When he argues, there is a scuffle and the words 'Sorry squire, I seem to have scratched the record' repeat ad infinitum in the run-out groove. A commentary on a Royal Festival Hall concert descending into mayhem is another new addition.

The extra sketches included on the US release were 'Communist Quiz' and 'Penguin On The TV', while others such as 'Spanish Inquisition' ran for longer.

Monty Python's Previous Record
Personnel:
Chapman, Cleese, Palin, Jones, Idle, Gilliam
Also appearing: Carol Cleveland, The Fred Tomlinson Singers, Neil Innes
Record Label: Charisma (UK), Buddah (US)
Recorded October 1972, produced by Michael Palin, Terry Jones, Andre Jacquemin and Alan Bailey.
Release date: December 1972 (UK), 1973 (US).
Chart Position: 39 (UK)
Running time: 45:23

Album Facts.
For the recording of their third album, the Pythons decamped to the Radio Luxembourg Studios in London for two days in October 1972. A mixture of previously aired sketches and new material, it contains a significant amount of material from the third series, as well as 'Fish License' from the second and one sketch ('Happy Valley') from the second German programme. One item, Idle's 'Radio Quiz Show', dates back to *I'm Sorry I'll Read That Again* when it was performed by Graeme Garden. The album was released midway through the UK broadcast of the third series and, probably as a result of this, almost all of the sketches featured are from the first half of that series. The exception is 'Dennis Moore', which appeared here first – a month before its TV debut.

Originally the second side of the album was planned to have three separate concentric grooves, so that the listener could hear any one of three random 'sides' depending on where the needle fell. This proved impossible when all of the grooves merged together midway through, so the plan was abandoned. According to sound engineer (and co-producer) Andre Jacquemin, this is why 'A Massage From The Swedish Prime Minister' appears three times – each separate groove was to start with this.

The original UK vinyl came with a single-sided 33rpm 'flexi-disc' (which had also been given away with issue 27 of *Zigzag* magazine) entitled *Teach Yourself Heath*, and containing directions on how to mimic the speech patterns of the then-prime minister. It was subsequently included as a bonus track on the 2006 CD 'special edition' reissue of the album. The album was also preceded by a single containing 'Eric The Half A Bee' on one side and 'Yangtze Song' on the other, with an extra 'karaoke version' of the latter. These tracks were, for some reason, mono versions of the stereo album tracks.

Album Cover.
The most 'Pythonesque' cover yet, this unmistakable Terry Gilliam design featured the title and picture almost entirely obscured by an arm, wrapping itself around the front and back several times, attempting to grasp a six-breasted woman/butterfly hybrid which is escaping it. The rear cover, which contained some black and white photographs, is also almost entirely obscured by the arm. Most of the photos are unrecognisable.

The inner sleeve showed sixteen fictitious album covers on one side, while the other contained the lyrics to 'The Yangtze Song', as part of a Yangtze Club Newsletter, handwritten and difficult to read notes about the album by 'Mrs Enid Dibley' and a 'do-it-yourself' sleeve note. Readers will no doubt remember that 'Gwen Dibley's Flying Circus' was a suggested name for the show. The fake albums illustrated include such delights as: The Sound Of Hip Injuries, More Hip Injuries (Painfully Yours), Sheffield United Sing Noel Coward, An Evening With Martin Bormann (And The Trio Los Paraguayos), Party Time by Princess 'Piano' Margaret, Norma Shearer Whistles Duane Eddy, Take-Over Ballads by Sister-Nazi Ltd and More Songs From The Goole And District Catholic River Wideners Club.

The inner sleeve also contains an erroneous reference to 'Summarize Proust Competition', which was recorded for the album but dropped. Initial UK pressings had a label which identified the first side as 'A-Side And Half B-Side', in reference to the song 'Eric The Half A Bee', while the other side was listed as 'This Side', and contained a series of teeth-cleaning instructions.

Material.
Probably the team's strongest album yet, it completes the transition from the first record, which was essentially a disjointed series of sketches from the show, to this fully realised comedy album constructed to flow seamlessly from beginning to end. There is a lot of material specially written for the album,

including Idle's 'Australian Table Wine' which is something of a classic of its kind. Other excellent original items include the brilliant concept of a solar eclipse getting radio coverage (from cricket commentators), 'The Wonderful World Of Sound', 'Funerals At Prestatyn' and the delightfully insane 'Silly Noises'. Of note is the fact that he sketches taken from the third series of the TV show are very well chosen for the way they work without the visuals, with 'Argument', 'Anne Elk' and 'How To Do It' particularly strong in the absence of visuals.

'Fish Licence' was the only sketch taken from an earlier series, but there is a reason for this. Following the list of Cleese's pets named Eric, it goes straight into the previously unreleased song 'Eric The Half A Bee', composed by Idle and Cleese and sung (or more accurately half-spoken) by Cleese. Neil Innes plays piano on the track. In fact, Cleese himself has said that the song was initially suggested as following 'Fish Licence' in the original episode, but he declined to do it, describing himself as 'most unmusical' by way of explanation. He has expressed his regret that they didn't use it in the TV show, retrospectively. One notable thing about the track is that it ends with the words 'semi carnally', which is 'misheard' by the backing Fred Tomlinson Singers as 'Cyril Connolly', an English writer and literary critic not exactly a household name to the average listener, it must be said. The correct words are explained to them, but they continue to sing 'Cyril Connolly' to the coda. Connolly died suddenly in 1974 at the age of 71, and this part of the song was edited out of future compilation appearances of it, but whether the two are linked is unclear.

The album closes with one item from the second of the team's German shows, the excellent 'Happy Valley'. It is a great shame that this hilarious fairy tale spoof never made it into the UK TV show, but it ends the album on a high note.

The Monty Python Matching Tie And Handkerchief

Personnel:
Chapman, Cleese, Palin, Jones, Idle, Gilliam
Also appearing: Carol Cleveland, Neil Innes
Record Label: Charisma (UK), Arista (US)
Recorded September 1973, produced by Andre Jacquemin, Dave Howman and Terry Gilliam.
Release date: December 1973 (UK), April 1975 (US).
Chart Position: 49 (UK)
Running time: 41:11

Album Facts.
Taking another step further away from the first album's 'cheaply packaged collection of sketches', *The Monty Python Matching Tie And Handkerchief* contained a lot of material newly written for the album. There were also a few sketches from the third series, one from the second and one from the first. The most notable thing about the original pressing of the vinyl album was that, finally making good on the aborted idea for the *Previous Record*, the second

side of the record contained two separate concentric grooves. This meant that depending where the needle dropped the listener could hear one of two 'sides' (though both were short, obviously, given the inherent capacity of twelve inches of vinyl). While this was a brilliantly original idea (it had been done much earlier for 78rpm discs, but never for a modern LP record), and certainly a talking (and selling) point, it was also one which wore thin fairly quickly. The obvious downside was that when the listener wanted to hear a particular set of material, he or she might have to repeatedly lift the arm on and off the record until happening to 'hit' the desired one. There is also the possibility that some unsuspecting listeners may never, or at least for some time, have even heard a significant portion of the record if the needle had never landed that way for them. All in all, originality gets a ten, practicality gets a much lower score!

In addition to this double-grooving, there was the added confusion that both sides of the label were identified as a free record given away with the tie and handkerchief set, and both also identified as Side Two. With no tracklisting anywhere, the potential for confusion was clearly quite large. The album was the first *Python* record to be mastered by George 'Porky' Peckham, who became notorious in the 1970s for adding etched messages in the run-out grooves, the most common being 'A Porky Prime Cut'. This album had 'Porky-Ray Adventure' for some hard to discern reason. Bizarrely, after being recorded at Luxembourg Studios, the album was mixed and edited in a garden shed belonging to producer Andre Jacquemin's father! Arthur 'Two-Sheds' Jackson would be proud...

The US release was delayed for almost eighteen months until April 1975, as the US record company changed to Arista, and was preceded by a single containing three excerpts and one full track.

Album Cover.
The most elaborate yet, this typically Gilliam-esque design has the outer cover as a die-cut sleeve with a hole in the front, inside which one could see the titular tie and handkerchief. Removing the insert sheet, however, revealed the full picture to be a man (wearing the matching items) being - quite graphically - lynched from a scaffold. A second insert featured the album credits as well as the text of the 'Background To History' sketch, along with another classic Gilliam illustration. All of this gave the album a real feel of being an original work – a 'real' album if you will – rather than the more usual collection of sketches which comedy albums would tend to be. This approach would influence other UK comics such as Billy Connolly, Mike Harding, Max Boyce and Jasper Carrott with their own record designs of the same time period.

Material.
The material on the 'normal' first side of the album is extremely strong, with some choice sketches combined with brilliant original material such as the 'Thomas Hardy Novel Writing' and 'Elephant Surgery', while the 'Bruces' sketch is, for the first time, combined with its now-inseparable coda, the

'Philosophers Song'. The 'double' side is a little weaker, however, with 'Boxing Night' in particular failing to work at all without the visuals. The routine around the record shop customer listening to an album entitled 'First World War Noises' is the pick of this half, but 'The Background To History', depicting historical events using reggae, pop and rock songs, struggles a little under its own weight, clever though it is, and the final 'Phone In' sketch drags somewhat. All in all, it's a very worthy album, if perhaps just a notch below *Monty Python's Previous Record* in quality.

Monty Python Live At Drury Lane

Personnel:
Chapman, Cleese, Palin, Jones, Idle, Gilliam
Also appearing: Lynn Ashley, Neil Innes
Record Label: Charisma (UK)
Recorded Live March 1974, produced by Andre Jacquemin, Dave Howman and Alan Bailey.
Release date: June 1974 (UK). Not released in US
Chart Position: 19 (UK)
Running time: 61:35

Album Facts.

The first 'true' *Python* live album (not counting the first record, which was really an excuse to get the scripts recorded with some laughter), and many still consider this the best. The album was recorded on the last night of a four week run at London's Theatre Royal, Drury Lane (obviously!), on 23 March 1974. Considering the *Holy Grail* film was being worked on at the time, as well as the writing of the fourth TV series, this month-long stint was an incredible amount of work.

The vinyl had another etched message by George 'Porky' Peckham – this time reading 'The wonderful world of Porky Trishy Melly Yeah!', on the run-out groove of the second side.

The record was the most successful *Python* album to date, reaching Number nineteen on the UK album chart. However, despite this, it was not given a US release until almost 30 years later, when it finally appeared as part of a CD box set, *The Instant Monty Python CD Collection*. It was, however, released in Canada in 1975. A '*Python* Special' edition of the music paper *New Musical Express* gave away a flexi-disc single called 'Monty Python's Tiny Black Round Thing', featuring some of the material from the album.

Carol Cleveland was not available to appear in the live show, so Idle's wife Lyn Ashley covered all of her roles.

Album Cover.

Less of a lavishly packaged affair than its recent predecessors, the cover for this was actually designed by Gilliam's assistant, Katy Hepburn (unfortunately she is misspelt as 'Hebbern' in the credits). It shows a stage with a lone spotlight picking out a TV set with the 'foot' on it. The back cover features some photos from the show, displayed on TV screens, along with some short but humorous credits and a tracklisting.

Material.
For the most part consisting of excellent renditions of some of the *Python* 'greatest hits' sketches, there are also major bonus delights featured here. Chief among those must be the immortal 'Four Yorkshiremen', which was an item on the *At Last The 1948 Show*, but so definitive is this version that people now generally assume it to be a *Python* sketch. The 'Cocktails' sketch, which was banned from the TV show, also turns up in all of its tasteless glory here, while 'Election Night Special' is extended from the TV version and much improved. Other pre-*Python* material included 'Secret Service' and 'Wrestling', while Neil Innes chips in with his song 'How Sweet To Be An Idiot', which was ruled to have been borrowed for the melody of the Oasis track 'Whatever', and for which Innes now receives royalties. There is also a Terry Gilliam-composed song entitled 'I've Got Two Legs'.

The Album of the Soundtrack of the Trailer of the Film of Monty Python and the Holy Grail
Personnel:
Chapman, Cleese, Palin, Jones, Idle, Gilliam
Also appearing: Mike Berry, The Fred Tomlinson Singers
Record Label: Charisma (UK), Arista (US)
Recorded March 1975 (new material), produced by Jones, Palin, Gilliam, Howman, Jacquemin
Release date: 18 July 1975 (UK), 21 July 1975 (US)
Chart Position: 45 (UK)
Running time: 57:44

Album Facts.
Typical of *Python* items of the time, this is as far from a straight soundtrack recording as you could get. It consists of some of the best scenes from the film, presented as if being shown at an actual theatre (The Classic, Silbury Hill). This includes a tour of the theatre, commentary about parts of the film which fail to work without the visuals and also comments entirely for the benefit of those buying the 'executive version' of the record, which of course didn't exist.

The album contained further George Peckham etchings in the run-out groove. On Side One it read 'An Executive Porky Prime Cut', while the other side was 'This is the small detailed writing on the album of the soundtrack of the trailer of the film of *Monty Python and the Holy Grail* – this writing is not included on the executive version of the soundtrack of the trailer of the film of *Monty Python and the Holy Grail*'. In small letters.

Album Cover.
The cover featured an eye-catching Gilliam design with the lengthy title in faux-3D lettering getting smaller as it disappears toward a rising red sun. The reverse had this picture partly torn away to reveal some very funny, if sadly brief, fake credits, including a large disclaimer that the record can only be played once.

Material.
As previously noted, this is much more than a mere soundtrack. In addition to the Silbury theatre showing and 'Executive Edition' running gags, there is a classic Cleese turn as a logician discussing the 'Witch' scene and getting distracted, live coverage from the London Premiere, with a multi-car actor pile-up outside and an interview with a film-maker, whose latest film includes a performance from Marilyn Monroe, despite her being dead. The part when the coconuts arrive for the first time is worth it alone! This is how all comedy soundtracks should be done.

The Monty Python Instant Record Collection.
Personnel:
Chapman, Cleese, Palin, Jones, Idle, Gilliam
Record Label: Charisma (UK). Arista (US)
Release date: 2 December 1977 (UK), 7 December 1981 (US)
Chart Position: Did not chart
Running time: 57:44

Album Facts.
The first *Python* compilation album, this is all previously released material from the Charisma albums, with a couple of slight changes and the 'Summarise Proust' sketch appearing on record for the first time. The record's chief interest is its extraordinary cover design. On the original release, the package was a folded cube, which when assembled made up an apparent collection of vinyl albums, with the front and back covers of this one at either end. The front cover had a sort of giant sausage being sliced into vinyl records (which have the Charisma label), while the back had the same knife slicing away a fake Tchaikovsky album (including some hilarious false sleeve-notes involving 'records for the hard of hearing') to reveal the tracklisting to the *Python* record.

The US release came four years later with a different tracklisting, drawn from the Arista US albums.

Monty Python's Life Of Brian
Personnel:
Chapman, Cleese, Palin, Jones, Idle, Gilliam

Record Label: Warner Brothers
Recorded August 1979 (new material), produced by Chapman, Idle, Howman, Jacquemin
Release date: 9 November 1979 (UK), 8 October 1979 (US)
Chart Position: 63 (UK)
Running time: 51:51

Album Facts.
This soundtrack album followed the template of the *Holy Grail* album, with new material linking the film clips, but less ambitiously and with less success. There is less new material this time and, while it is of good quality, this does not make the record quite as indispensable to those very familiar with the film. Only Idle and Chapman are involved in the new material. The design is also less ambitious, with a front cover based on the film poster, a rear cover with lots of headshots from the film and a tracklisting, with an inner sleeve having a collage of monochrome stills from the film.

The Monty Python Contractual Obligation Album
Personnel:
Chapman, Cleese, Palin, Jones, Idle
Also appearing: Mike Berry, The Fred Tomlinson Singers
Record Label: Charisma (UK), Arista (US)
Recorded January-May 1980), produced by Eric Idle, Andre Jacquemin
Release date: 6 October 1980 (UK), 7 October 1980 (US)
Chart Position: 13 (UK)
Running time: 46:23

Album Facts.
A joke title, yet one which has its basis in fact, as the Pythons owed Charisma Records one further album, following the *Life Of Brian* soundtrack, which came out on Warner Bros. Nevertheless, that isn't to say that the album is a shoddy affair, thrown together for the sake of it. The material was all either new or redone from other *Python*-related projects. There is much more in the way of songs than usual, but whether that is positive or negative is in the ear of the listener.

The album actually achieved their highest UK chart position of thirteen, partly aided by Michael Palin's appearance on the BBC show *Top Of The Pops* to help promote it. He introduced the single 'Dog Eat Dog' by Adam And The Ants. The usual Porky Peckham etchings were present, this time reading 'Excuse the pause between sides, we've just nipped out to the pub for a pint' on side one, and 'Dear mum, please send another cuppa down, still cutting the *Python* LP. Love Porky X' on the reverse.

All of the group, with the exception of Gilliam, were included on the album. Cleese is only on three tracks, but this is partly due to the large amount of material recorded but not used.

Album Cover.

No Gilliam this time, as the front cover merely has a photograph of a plain paper inner sleeve with the title stamped on it. He is mentioned, however, as there is writing on this sleeve from Palin asking 'Can T.G. do a nice-eye catching cover to help it sell?', to which Jones adds the reply 'Not really worth it'. Note that the record label visible on the cover has a fake label, with a tracklisting referring to the contractual status of the recording. The actual inner sleeve had hand-scribbled 'credits', while the record labels are made to look as if part of them had been torn off and hand-written with 'Side One' and 'The Other Side'.

The cover design was by Basil Pao, who had worked on the book which accompanied *Life Of Brian*, and later went on to be the stills photographer for Palin's travel documentaries.

Material.

This is very much a mixed bag. Some of the material was from pre-Python days ('String' was originally performed by Ronnies Barker and Corbett on *The Frost Report*, while 'Bookshop' dates from *At Last The 1948 Show*, but that is fine because it was little remembered by this time, of good quality and new to most listeners. What is of more concern is the sheer volume of songs on the album; well over half of the material, in fact. *Python* had always involved occasional musical items, but these were very much the exception – this redressed the balance too far, and too much in the direction of both Jones and, especially, Idle. Some of the songs are good, including the sheer offensiveness of 'Never Be Rude To An Arab' and the classic travel-agency spoof of 'Finland', but items such as 'I'm So Worried', 'Muddy Knees' and 'Traffic Lights' border on the painful. About half of the album is worthwhile, which for the last newly-recorded *Python* studio album, is nowhere near good enough.

The original cassette had a long gap at the end of Side One, with Side Two being several minutes longer, so after 'I'm So Worried' mercifully finished, this medium has a five minute gap before Idle comes in announcing that this is the end of the silence and the tape can be turned over. Which would hardly cause a stampede for 'new material', one suspects. The song 'Here Comes Another One' is sung by Mike Berry, a '60s singer who went on to play Mr Spooner in the TV show *Are You Being Served*. The track 'Farewell To John Denver' had a convoluted life: it consists of a little snatch of a parody of 'Annie's Song' followed by Denver being strangled. This was withdrawn in the UK after the first pressings, whether because of questionable taste or licensing – opinions differ. It was reinstated, before being unsurprisingly withdrawn again after Denver's death in a plane crash. Who knows what the future holds for this hardly-worth-it-in-the-first-place joke?

Monty Python's The Meaning Of Life

Personnel:

Chapman, Cleese, Palin, Jones, Idle, Gilliam

Record Label: CBS (UK), MCA (US)
Recorded 1983 (new material), produced by Michael Palin, Andre Jacquemin,
Release date: 20 June 1983 (UK), 5 April 1993 (US).
Chart Position: did not chart
Running time: 53:17

Album Facts.

This soundtrack album has a similar approach to Life Of Brian, albeit with further diminishing returns with less new material than ever (all by Palin, with a brief Gilliam appearance). All of the songs from the film are included in full. The front cover is quite eye-catching, showing a grand-looking illustration of the tombstone being etched with the title, while the reverse shows the fish, along with the song credits and some amusing notes about it being marketed as a Philosophy album, but it all feels rather as if the spirit had gone, sadly.

Epilogue: Other Bits and What Came Next...

In addition to the TV shows, the records and the films, the other avenue which the *Python* creative team strayed into in the '70s was that of books. This was common practice at the time since, before the advent of video recorders, books were the only way to recapture the visual element of such programmes - The Goodies had their own, similar volumes around the same time.

The first such book to appear was *The Monty Python Big Red Book*, in 1971, which of course came with a blue cover. Nowadays it seems unremarkable, with most of the content based around items from the first two series of *Flying Circus*, but back then it was the 'thing' to be seen with. If someone had a copy at a UK school in the early '70s, they were an object of almost reverence! The initial hardback printing came with a sticker reading 'Very Urgent' on the front, but the paperback edition predictably replaced that with the words 'Special New Hardback Edition'. In an ultimate act of 'nerd cool', the book was referenced in the 2008 *Doctor Who* episode 'Silence In The Library'.

Following this in 1973, came *The Brand New Monty Python Bok* (Later *Papperbok* in the paperback edition). This was an improvement in terms of content as much of it was brand new material, with even a lot of the TV-inspired stuff only loosely derived from the original items. It came in a dust jacket with realistic dirty fingerprints on (later reproduced on the paperback cover), with the actual book cover within featuring a magazine entitled 'Tits 'n' Bums', which was designed as a sort of pornographic church magazine, earning howls of complaint. This led to one amusing story from the publisher Geoffrey Strachan, who related that one elderly lady bookseller wrote to complain about the fingerprints. On being told they were intended to be there, she retorted 'well, I shall sell it without the jacket then', and slammed the phone down – clearly having not yet looked at what was within!

One final book of note was that accompanying the *Life Of Brian* film. *Holy Grail* gave rise to a book of the screenplay, but the *Brian* combined screenplay and 'scrapbook' was chock-full of original and extremely funny content. It's well worth tracking down a copy of it – but ensure you get the 1979 original, as a screenplay-only book with an identical cover design was published in 2002. I know this because I bought it by accident.

After the scope of this book ends, with the final film in 1983, most of the *Python* team went on to notable extracurricular success with various film and TV projects. Cleese starred in a string of hugely successful films, such as *Clockwise*, *A Fish Called Wanda*, *Fierce Creatures* and, more recently, even acclaimed turns in the Harry Potter and James Bond franchises. He has guest-starred in a host of other films, normally when the material interests him. Michael Palin initially plunged himself into film work (*A Private Function*, *Brazil*, *American Friends*, plus appearances with Cleese in *Wanda* and *Fierce Creatures*), but soon became a household name for his enormously acclaimed travel documentaries. Idle had some film success with movies like *Splitting Heirs*, *Nuns On The Run* and *National Lampoon's European Vacation*, but none of these made essential viewing, and he moved into voiceover work. Terry Gilliam went on to massive success in directing and writing, indulging his visual creativity and imagination with the likes of *Brazil, Baron Munchausen, The Fisher King* and *12 Monkeys*. Terry Jones had some success in film (often behind the camera) in the '80s and '90s, but also made a name for himself as a writer of books, many for children and in the fantasy realm, but also serious historical works. Sadly, in recent years he has become afflicted with a form of dementia which has rendered him unable to speak since around 2017, according to Palin. Graham Chapman was the saddest case, only having one major solo project, that being the critically savaged *Yellowbeard* in 1983. From then he had only a few roles before he passed away in 1989 from Cancer.

There have been several notable celebrations, for anniversaries and the like, over the years, including 20th and 30th anniversary compilations entitled, respectively, *Parrot Sketch Not Included* and the imaginative *Python Night*. The former – which sure enough did not include the Parrot Sketch – was a collection of sketches from mainstream *Python* and the German *Fliegender Zirkus* shows, and was introduced by Steve Martin. The latter actually included some new material written for the 30th anniversary celebration, most of which Eric Idle announced was terrible, though the rest were guardedly happy, and some interesting documentaries. It's worth seeking out, but special mention must go to Carol Cleveland addressing a 'sexism' focus group including the Gumbys, some women and Ghandi, a new Gilliam animation in which a Buddhist kills chickens with multiplication, and the BBC2 announcers rebelling and changing the channel name to BBC1 followed by the closing BBC announcement that it is closing forever. It didn't.

Perhaps best of all is *Monty Python's Personal Best*, from 2006, which consisted of six hour long specials with each member presenting their favourite sketches which they wrote or appeared in, together with new material, and the five collaborating on one for Chapman. John Cleese's show features the revelation that he is 96 years old and ends with his death; Terry Gilliam's reveals the fact that he is himself an animation; Eric Idle interviews people about the show (including a former Nazi living in South America, played by himself) and continually confuses the team with the Beatles; Michael Palin's show is in the form of a documentary about fish-slapping; finally, Jones announces he invented the show entirely by himself and that 'Monty Python' is, in fact, an anagram of 'Terry Jones'.

There have been sporadic *Python* stage reunions over the years, even after Chapman's death, with the most notable being the *Live At Aspen* show from 1998 featuring a mock interview and the final *Monty Python Live (Mostly)* from the O2 in London, 2104 – the first group appearance performing actual sketches for 34 years, together with guest appearances. These should be watched with a hint of melancholy as, with the inability of Jones to take part any further owing to ill health, there will be no more. We must cherish them through the huge legacy left to us in the TV and film work celebrated within these pages.

We will not see their like again.

Appendix:

The full list of those fake album spines from *The Monty Python Instant Record Collection*:

Rock and Roll Is Here to Stay Again!
The Beatles Chauffeurs Live!
Running Songs and Surrendering Ballads:
The Massed Bands of the Queen's Own
Cowards (or Some of Them)
Eternally Yours - The Massed Windscale
Marching Scientists
Ron Simon and Geoff Garfunkel - Live
from the Tennis Club Purley
Together Again - Frank and Ifield
My Brain Hurts - The Moron Tabernacle
Choir
The Milkman Whistles Stockhausen - 'A'
Milkman
When We're Apart - The Legs
Friday Night Is Bath Night - J.P.Gumby
When the Chickens Are Asleep - Ramon
and Ted
Nixon's Solid Gold Denials
Norma Shearer Whistles Duane Eddie
Teach Yourself Power
The Best Bits of Rolf Harris
Monty Python's Best Sketches Beginning
With 'R'
Hitting Ourselves with the Little Curved
Bit on the End of the Shaving Brush - Eric
and the Loonies
My Brain Hurts and Other National Front
Marching Songs
The Best Of The Osmonds' Teeth Vol XI
An Evening with Martin Bormann (and the
Trio los Paraguayos)
A Night In Casablanca - The Everly Sisters
Give Me the Moonlight and the Goats -
Ramon and Ted
A Man Who Once Sold Paul McCartney A
Newspaper - LIVE!
RAW POWER PUNK KILL BLAST
THROTTLE DESTROY - Clodagh Rotten
The Dave Clark Five's War Speeches
The Best of Reggae Maudling (Rastatory
Label)
The Wonderful Sound of Hip Injuries
Beethoven's Punk Symphony, in B
Flat - "The Stinking Bastard" (Bandages
Supplied)
The Horrid Brothers Kill Anyone in Sight
Party Time - Princess "Piano" Margaret
Young, Gifted, Black and Furry - Ramon

and Ted
My Way Or Else - Frank Sinatra
It's All Over My Friend - Earl K Vomit and
the Meatabolic Processes
John, Paul, George, and Ringo - The
Davenport Brothers
Scottish Airs - the Hamish McFart Singers
I Left My Pacemaker In San Francisco - Dr
DeBakey
More Songs From the Goole and District
Catholic River Wideners Club
Bernard Delfont Live at the Bank Next to
the London Palladium
Bright Lights, Soft Music, Live Goats -
Ramon and Ted
Footloose And Fancy Free - Britt Eckland
A Night On The Town - Britt Eckland
Smiler - Britt Eckland
Gasoline Alley - Britt Eckland
Never A Dull Moment - Britt Eckland
An Old Raincoat Won't Ever Let You Down
- Britt Eckland
Every Picture Tells A Story - Britt Eckland
Atlantic - Britt Eckland
Every Picture Tells A Story - Britt Eckland
Rastaman – Sir Keith Joseph (Deleted)
I've Got a Beer Glass Sticking in My Head
and Other Rugby Songs
Accountants' Work Songs
Ruling Songs and Ballads - H.M. The
Queen and the Jordanaires
I'm in the Mood for Love and Goats and
Chickens - Ramon and Ted
Pet Smells - The Beach Boys
Monty Python Tries It On Again
BING IS BACK!
BACK IS BING!
BANG GOES BOING!
BONG BANGY BING!
BOEING BOEING (Cast Album)
Tom Jones Hits Frank Sinatra While Vic
Damone and Mel Torme Grab Engelbert
Humperdinck, at Las Vegas
YOU and THE NIGHT and THE MUSIC
and THE CHICKEN: Ramon and Ted
Get Bach - The Best of the Welsh Beatles
The Pick of the Best of Some Recently
Repeated Python Hits Again Vol II

Bibliography

Palin, M., *Diaries 1969-79: The Python Years* (W&N, 2006)

Ross, R., *The Monty Python Encyclopedia* (Batsford, 2001)

Larson, D., *Monty Python's Flying Circus: An Utterly Complete, Thoroughly Unillustrated, Absolutely Unauthorized Guide to Possibly All the References* (Scarecrow, 2008)

Idle, E., *The Rutland Dirty Weekend Book* (Mandarin, 1976)

Clayson, A., *George Harrison* (Part of Beatles Box Set, Sanctuary, 2003)

Python, M., *The Monty Python Big Red Book* (Methuen, 1971)

Python, M., *The Brand New Monty Python Bok* (Methuen, 1973)

Python, M., *Life Of Brian: Monty Python's Scrapbook* (Methuen, 1979)

Johnson, K,. *And Now For Something Completely Trivial* (St Martins Press, 1991)